# NORTH STREET ☞ BRISTOL

## SHOPS, SHOPPING AND SHOPPERS

By John Holland,
Pat Hooper & Martin Howard

First published in 2015 by Tangent Books

Tangent Books, Unit 5.16 Paintworks, Bristol BS4 3EH

**www.tangentbooks.co.uk**
**Tel: 0117 972 0645**

**Publisher:** Richard Jones (richard@tangentbooks.co.uk)

**Design:** Joe Burt (joe@wildsparkdesign.com)

**ISBN:** 978-1-910089-17-0

A CIP catalogue record for this book is available from the British Library

Printed on paper from sustainable sources.

*In memory of Anton Bantock, whose lifelong enthusiasm for bringing south Bristol's history to life in words and illustrations has been an inspiration to the authors.*

*Dedicated to all the shopkeepers of North Street, past and present.*

# CONTENTS

# FOREWORD

I have known North Street for the past 30 years or so, firstly as an architect when I worked up proposals for the conversion of the massive Imperial Tobacco Estate to a mixture of uses, but my close association began in 1993 when I bought the pile of red bricks, on the corner of Raleigh Rd and North St, known as the Franklyn Davey building or 'No2 factory'. This was in order to give it a new lease of life, but was also a vain attempt to save its more magnificent five storey neighbours, including the WD & HO Wills 'No3 factory'. Not being able to afford a quick conversion, I developed what was to become known as the Tobacco Factory over a period of seven years, opening the café-bar in 2001. Above it we created a raw theatre space, dance studio, work and living space and a fitness gym. A thriving local market, now held every Sunday in the former works yard, has helped to complete the picture, along with the Bristol Beer Factory, Mark's Bakery and a second theatre and dance space down the road. Whilst I take pride in the outcome, which has exceeded my expectations, the Tobacco Factory is just one of a number of factors that have contributed to the revival of North Street – some of which are related in this book.

This revealing book charts the history of retail along North Street, beginning in the days when shopping locally was the norm and independent traders were the retail kings and queens. Like countless similar streets in towns and cities across the country, North Street suffered decades of decline with trade severely hit by the introduction of national supermarket chains which heralded a major change in shopping habits. The final straw for Bedminster was when Imperial Tobacco transferred its workforce to a vast modern factory near Hartcliffe, taking away substantial local purchasing power. By the 1980s, much of North Street had an air of neglect with numerous properties standing empty and forlorn.

However, in recent years an impressive fight-back – helped by impressive support from the North Street Traders' Association, and most recently by establishing a Business Improvement District – has gathered momentum and I am delighted that North Street is now held up as a shining example both in Bristol and beyond of a community shopping area which has bucked the trend. Local shops are once again on the radar of many who live in the area, as well as those who come from further afield. Independent traders are largely thriving, for the first time in three or four decades. A wide variety of shops along many parts of the street are in full occupancy, there's an intriguing mix of old and new, including a near saturation of restaurants, cafés and bars!

To help tell the story of North Street, the authors have drawn together recollections and experiences of countless people – shopkeepers, shop workers and shoppers alike. This book is more than just about shops. For some local residents, several generations of their family have lived, worked and shopped here, while others just drop by. What all these people have in common, and what is very apparent from all their stories, is their love of North Street and the community that it represents. My hope for the future of North Street is that it reinforces its distinctive local independent culture, that it provides a genuine alternative to the bland superstores and becomes the natural meeting place for all who are fortunate enough to live and work nearby. This book invites readers to form their own vision for local shopping. Long may North Street flourish!

**George Ferguson**
*Mayor of Bristol*

# INTRODUCTION

**N**orth Street, situated in south Bristol, is a ribbon of shops and houses stretching from the heart of Bedminster to the neighbouring suburb of Ashton. Along its mile length can be found a range of shops, cafés, restaurants and pubs – some thriving, others less so; recent arrivals, as well as several businesses with long and illustrious histories. North Street is typical of suburban shopping areas in towns and cities across the country and like many similar high streets its fortunes have waxed and waned over the years.

This book is all about shops – shops that draw us in, sometimes from necessity, other times on impulse as we stroll down our local high street. Shops that may also tell us something of the past and how our community once shopped. Whatever the purpose of our visit, our memories of particular shops, visited on a regular basis or for a special reason, often include the people who worked there and the way in which they served us.

When work started on this book our aim was to include every building currently a shop, as well as buildings which were once, but no longer, shops – whether bombed, converted to a different use or just lying empty. In the case of shops still in operation, shopkeepers were remarkably candid about current trade, the state of retail shopping in North Street and what the future holds.

What is a shop? Perhaps a working definition could be: a place where you go to buy something, to be fed, entertained or 'served' in some way. That is why, as well as places where you might take your shopping bag, you will find five pubs included here, as well as a theatre and former cinemas, petrol stations, laundries, banks and a tattoo parlour – not forgetting North Street's defining 'shop' of the current decade, the numerous cafés, bars and restaurants. We admit to straying from our own definition: how could we not mention North Street's connection with a notorious multi-million pound robbery, the ladder maker whose firm traded here for more than 80 years, or the poets Wordsworth and Southey? We apologise for being unable to include the taxi firm, the primary school, several estate agents and other places – material for a further book perhaps. Our choices for inclusion were determined partly by our definition of a shop, partly by the people who came forward with their stories. We were especially keen to speak to retired shopkeepers and record their tales, willingly told, of a lifetime in trade. Our intention is not to take a sentimental look at better times. However, we hope that readers of the book, whether they know the area, or shop in a similar street elsewhere, will feel a connection with what is described here and recognise the importance of 'the everyday' in all our lives.

The book is set out so as to take the reader on a 'walk' – up one side of North Street and back down the other. Each chapter describes the various premises along a particular stretch of North Street between the side roads leading off it. Where we were able to gather a wealth of information about a particular premises, past or current, this appears as a feature shop. Readers seeking a favourite location can either find it via its number in the street, or search the index which also provides a list of names of the people who appear throughout the book.

Inevitably this book presents a snapshot of the businesses along North Street at a particular moment in their history and we realise that changes will have taken place since the time of writing. All books which are based on memories are bound to contain a few inaccuracies where recollections fade over time, and we apologise if any mistakes or omissions cause offence.

The authors are indebted to the hundred or so people who came forward and volunteered their stories, photographs, sketch maps showing where the shops were, as well as other memorabilia. What these people – whether shop owners, workers or shoppers – have in common, and what is very apparent in all their stories, is their enduring commitment to North Street and passionate belief that it has a secure future.

# NORTH STREET –
# A BRIEF HISTORY

NORTH STREET - A BRIEF HISTORY

**U**ntil the early 1900s, North Street was a route, not a destination. Visitors, and farmers with their produce, would travel along the Ashton Road turnpike from as far as Brockley in Somerset, pay their dues at the Ashton Gate toll house and then reach Bedminster a mile further east. Those travelling from the south of Bristol on the toll road from Dundry and the Mendip Hills would pass through the Luckwell Lane toll gate which was situated at the top of the current Luckwell Road to join North Street about half way along, near the Hen and Chicken public house. Thus two important toll roads led to and from North Street, and from this junction North Street descended eastwards into Bedminster. The 'road of two halves' that our twentieth century shoppers have highlighted was in fact an old division marked by this junction at the Hen and Chicken inn.

When John Wesley preached here in the 1760s, Bedminster was a sprawling and decayed market town, with orchards, brickworks, rope-walks and cottage industries. However, all this was to change with the development of the south Bristol coalfields and the population jumped from 3,000 in 1801 to 78,000 in 1884 as people from depressed rural Somerset flocked to the expanding coal mines for work. Almost overnight Bedminster became a power-house of heavy industry, manned by a huge workforce which was packed into high-density terraced housing. Coal mining and smelting generated other industries: engineering, tanneries, glue-works, paint factories and glassworks. In the 1880s, ES & A Robinson's paper-bag business and WD & HO Wills' tobacco business moved to new factories in Bedminster.

## FASHIONABLY RURAL

**The 1828 map shows that before the industrial boom North Street was still a rural road.** In its eastern half a few rows of houses and cottages can be seen, as well as larger properties such as Carlton Place [still standing, numbers 186-192] and Bedminster House. To the west, though, there are few buildings except for one or two cottages. Of the public houses, the Star Inn and the Hen and Chicken are still in existence. All of the land northwards towards the river Avon, later to become Victorian Southville, is fields and orchards.

13

In the next three decades the eastern half of North Street (nearest Bedminster) was becoming a desirable 'out of town' place to live, away from the Bedminster slums, for those whose money was made from the local industries and the merchant sea trade. Thomas Hassell, Mayor and Sheriff of Bristol, lived in Bedminster House. In the 1820s, Bedminster justice was administered quite separately from that of Bristol. It had its own 'Petty Session' for offences such as 'absentee apprentices,' or 'drinking during the hours of divine service,' and Hassell would have been the magistrate presiding at both the Petty and the Quarter Sessions [for more serious cases] in the Star public house [numbers 4-6], just over the road from his house. Bookseller Joseph Cottle moved from the city to a new home in Carlton Terrace in 1832. The house was Carlton Place, one of the houses in what was by the 1850s to become a terrace of five Georgian homes set back from the road. Cottle was a minor poet, but was more famous as the publisher and publicist for the poets Southey and Coleridge when they were struggling to get into print, and also, later, for Wordsworth.

## PUBLIC HOUSES

**By the 1850s North Street was continuing to be developed in the eastern half towards Bedminster, with the construction of terraces such as Ashton Place and Albert Place [still standing, numbers 181-185].**

Even by 1870, North Street was still mainly a thoroughfare. It had a number of homes but only a handful of traders, such as a greengrocer, tea dealer and wheelwright, and they were outnumbered by the public houses. Of these the Star, Full Moon, Spotted Cow and the Hen and Chicken still survive. The White Lion stood almost opposite the current Masonic Hotel, and the Rose and Crown was replaced with houses in the 1880s.

## SUBURBAN

**By the 1880s one of the lords of the manor, Sir Greville Smyth, had started to develop Southville, and the eastern half of North Street was becoming well-served with rows of shops for the new residents.** The larger properties such as Dorset House, Luckwell House and Bedminster House were still standing and smaller industries were also still in operation, such as the Imperial Brewery adjacent to Bedminster House. There was even a coal pit, known as Northside Colliery or Goldstone's Pit, on the corner of South Street.

By 1900, almost all of the older landmark 'country houses' such as Bedminster House and North House had gone. The gated entrance to the rebuilt Wesleyan Chapel (erected in 1886 'by the removal of a cottage', according to newspaper reports) still stands today, but most of the older premises, as well as the remaining roadside land, had been replaced with terraces running between each street corner; these are

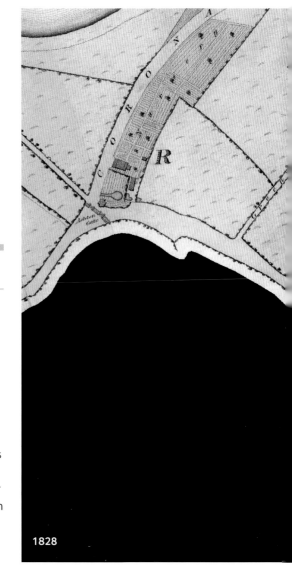

1828

the shops described in this book, along with the occasional run of terraced houses.

The last section of rural land to be developed was the western half of North Street, from the Ashton toll gate, as the 1903 map shows. At this end the old Ashton Brewery, the new Ashtongate [sic] school and St. Francis's Church

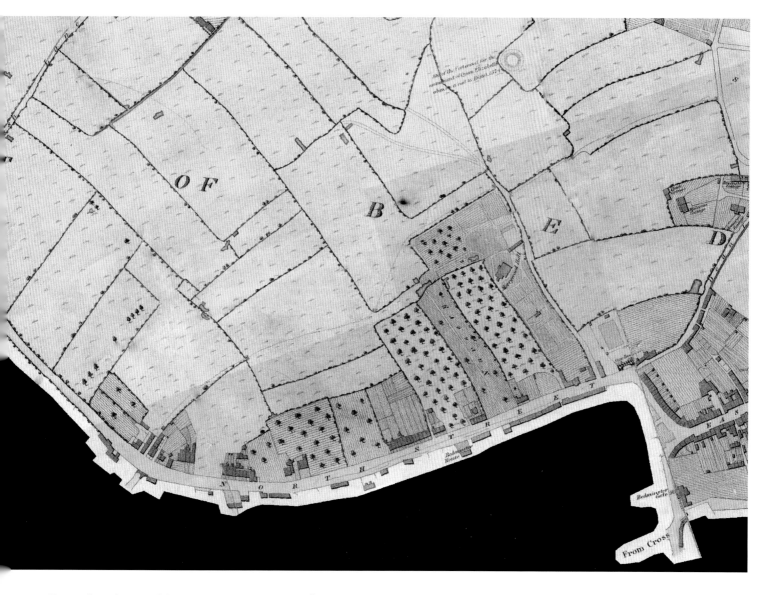

(formerly Holy Cross) became the landmarks, the gaps rapidly being filled between here and the Hen and Chicken with gabled, purpose-built shops and later, a cinema. With the new Franklyn Davey Tobacco Factory then being built around the turn of the century (erected on the site of Bedminster cricket ground), the whole street, now lined with buildings on both sides of its

mile's length, was ready to supply the Edwardians with almost all their retail, educational, work and spiritual needs.

There are only four 'listed' buildings in North Street, though the List does not contain all of the old surviving buildings in North Street. At the west end are the Ashton toll house and Ashton Gate School, built around 1820 and 1876 respectively. In the centre of North

Street, No 192 (currently a solicitors' office) was built around 1780. This abuts a short terrace of Georgian houses, although these are not listed. The least noticeable of the oldest buildings is number 49. Adjacent to the current Full Moon public house, it was built in the late 1600s. It became the New Inn, was renamed the Artichoke and then the Full Moon, which later moved next door to its

**15**

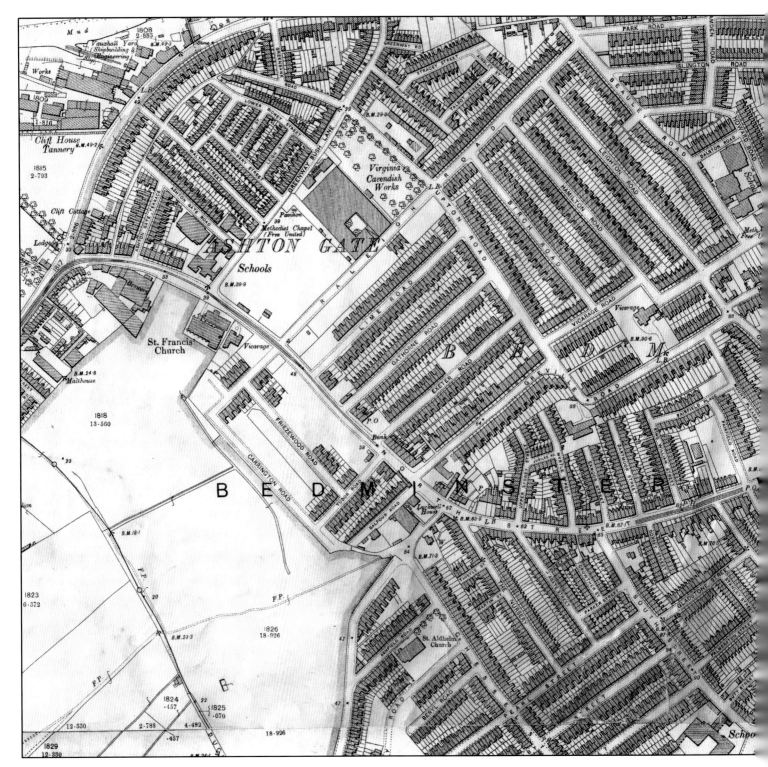

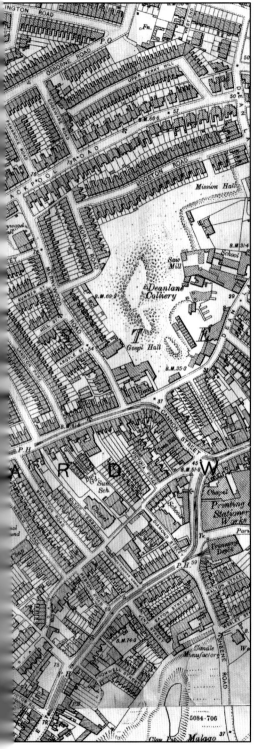

1885

current location at number 51.

This history has two further episodes. Wartime air-raids, from bombs misdirected or jettisoned en route to Bristol's docks, caused deaths and damage to the whole area. The book includes personal reminiscences of St. Francis's church in flames, and the Hen and Chicken pub was gutted, as can be seen in photographs elsewhere in this book. The biggest areas of destruction in North Street were in the eastern half. The stretch between Exmoor Road and King William Street was bombed, and these frontages became used-car sites and a petrol filling station after the war. Only since the rise in land value in the early years of the twenty first century have these plots been developed, but as housing, not shops. The other side of North Street here was hit too, to be replaced by the Bristol City Council Housing Department's Gaywood House tower block in the early 1960s. The corner of Luckwell Road and The Nursery was also destroyed, eventually becoming 'North Street Green'.

## WILLS' GIRLS

**With the arrival of supermarkets and 'shopping in town' in the 1960s, North Street's shops struggled to compete.** However, our research shows that this was still a prosperous street, if only because of the 'footfall' of the local population, especially the workers at the Wills' cigarette factories, the so-called 'Wills' Girls'. However, when the Bedminster and Ashton Gate Wills' factories were closed and production

moved to a new factory in Hartcliffe in 1974, the shoppers no longer swamped the local shops during their lunch break, or formed queues that stretched around the corner at the post office at Christmas, and the shopkeepers didn't need to stay open late on the factory's bonus day. In the words of Peter Budd of Pen Corner (12), 'Overnight the girls spending ten shillings were gone and their mothers spending sixpence were left.'

## NEW SHOPS

**North Street was not alone in suffering from the years of stagnation and decline which took their toll on a number of once-prosperous shopping streets in this part of south Bristol – nearby West Street being a prime example.** Several of the shopkeepers interviewed for this book describe the struggle to make ends meet during this period. However, in recent years North Street has undergone a revival and a sense of resurgence is now very apparent. New shops have opened and have quickly established strong reputations in the local community; other long-established shops have successfully managed to change with the times.

This rejuvenation and the accompanying sense of optimism have been helped by several factors. Firstly, the changing demographics of this part of Bristol, in particular, an influx of younger, professional workers with disposable incomes and the accompanying 'gentrification' of the

Victorian and Edwardian terraced houses which typify suburbs such as Ashton, Southville and Bedminster. Secondly, one of the few original cigarette factory buildings, originally owned by Messrs Franklyn Davey, has been converted into a very successful café/bar and nationally acclaimed performance venue, The Tobacco Factory. Thirdly, and somewhat ironically, given the negative impact of supermarkets on local shops from the 1950s onwards, three small supermarkets, each operated by a major company, have also played a part in the regeneration of the area by providing additional choice to people who shop locally. In addition, North Street once again has an active traders' association which organises several events during the year, the aim being to celebrate and promote shopping in the area. A Sunday market organised by The Tobacco Factory and originally held monthly has been so successful that it now takes place every week. The Bristol Pound is flourishing in its aim of supporting independent traders and the local currency can be used in the Tobacco Factory and over a dozen other North Street shops.

In 1897, butcher, poet and developer Aldred Collard wrote to Bristol Corporation seeking permission to demolish his slaughter house in North Street and replace it with shops and houses. In his letter he argued that 'more commodious premises will be more sanitary, as North Street is a business street and will become the principal one in Bedminster.' Although today there is little space left in North Street to build further 'commodious premises', 120 years after Mr Collard made his prediction, it has come true. Our research and the stories recorded in this book show how much external factors affect local high street shopping, but it seems that for the foreseeable future, North Street will continue to flourish.

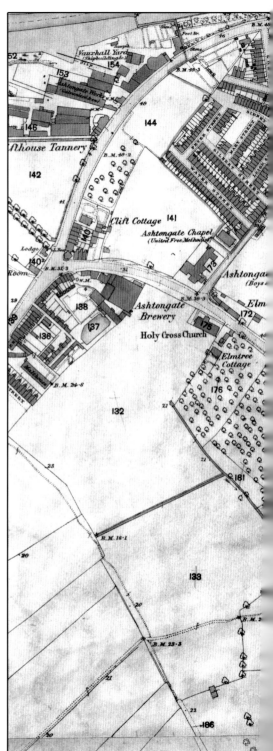

1903

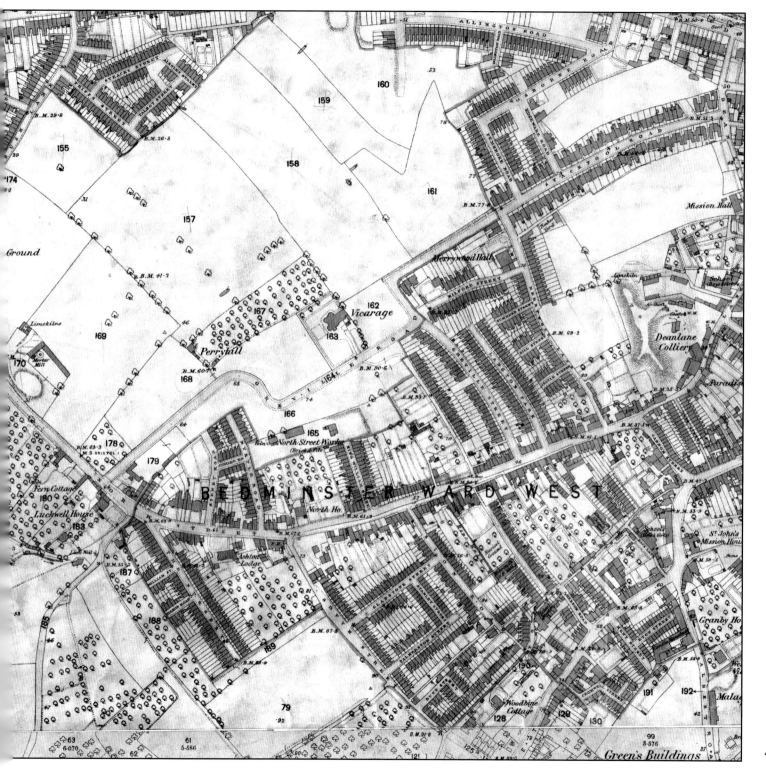

# A WALK ALONG NORTH STREET

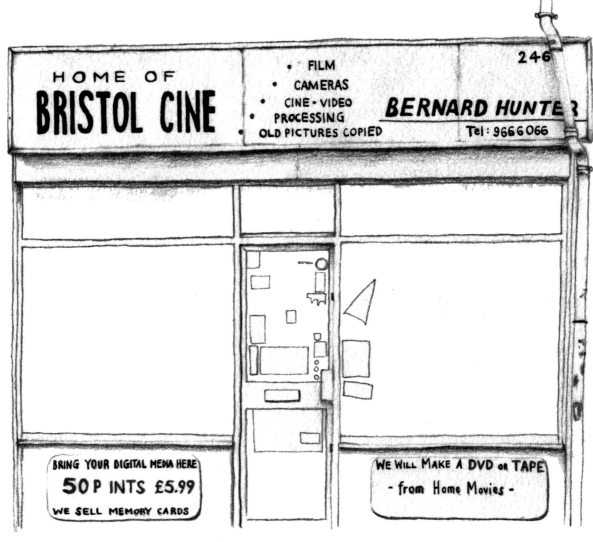

# CANNON STREET TO BRAUNTON ROAD 1-55

Tom Ward Clarke's drapers is the last shop in Cannon Street. 'Doctor' flannel, the trademark of a Rochdale textile firm, was popular in the first twenty years of the twentieth century.

**L**eaving the heart of Bedminster, North Street begins at a mini roundabout which forms a junction with Cannon Street and Dean Lane. The first few shops along North Street are housed in part of a curved terrace, built in the early years of the twentieth century and by 1910 the following shops were operating: Mrs Elizabeth Moden, pork butcher; Mrs Amelia Barnes, confectioner; Eastman's Ltd, butchers; Walter Henry Butt, grocer; Thomas Jenkins, baker; John Bessant, confectioner; Mrs Caroline Harvey, beer retailer.

Jeff Coleman remembers shopping in Butt's:

*My mother always bought her groceries on a Friday from Butt's. There were two counters, the one on the left was the butter counter. Mr Marker, the manager, would take a small knob of butter on a knife and offer it to my mother to taste and he would also offer her some cheese. There was bacon and ham and other goods on that counter. When the purchases were all packed on that side we moved to the dry goods side where the tea, sugar, coffee, biscuit and currants etc were sold.*

Several of these shops remained under the same management for many years, Moden's and Eastman's still going strong in the 1960s. In 2014, this terrace is home to a gift shop, two beauty lounges and a second-hand furniture shop, the latter in premises which have changed little since the days when it was the popular bakers, Pitt's (**see 9**). One of numerous small bakers along North Street at various times over the years, the business was affectionately known by customers as 'Pitties'. As well as selling bread and cakes, Pitt's provided a service for local residents as Jeff Coleman recalls: 'On Saturdays, my mother would make a bread pudding in a roasting tin that was too large to go into her oven so I was told to take it to Pitt's. They put the pudding in the oven with the loaves to cook. I was told to call back, in an hour's time and when I collected it, I paid 2d.'

Wartime bombing destroyed numbers 11 to 17, rebuilt soon after the war in a squat, 'four square' style using brick with steel-framed windows, for 20 years or so housing McDavid's Ltd, furniture dealers. A road-widening scheme for the Cannon Street junction is apparently the reason why this block was set back from the road, the plan being to eventually demolish numbers 1 to 9. Like many similar road schemes, this one came to nothing. Prior to the Second World War, a draper's shop stood on this site. In 2014, the shop is vacant and boarded up (**see 11-13**).

In January 2014, work finally began to build new homes and shops on the site formerly occupied by the Rex Cinema. The Rex (**see 19-25**) was built in 1939, damaged during an air raid during the Second World War, but quickly repaired and reopened. At one time the manager was Mr E G Handford, 'a very smart man' recalls Phil Elliot.

Next to the site where The Rex once stood is a distinctive russet brown building, currently the offices of Barcan Woodward, solicitors (**see 27-31**). The building probably dates from the mid-nineteenth century, one of a handful which survive from the period when North Street was little more than a lane leading out of Bristol on its south west edge from the (then) village of Bedminster. Although the 1870 street directory lists nine different trades operating along the entire length of what is now North Street – as well as six public houses, five of which still survive – it is impossible to tell with any degree of certainty who occupied number 27 and for what purpose.

The land adjacent to Barcan Woodward, now used as a car park, was the site of Jubilee Place and Berkeley Square. Little is known of these roads which almost certainly consisted of humble dwellings, perhaps occupied by workers at the nearby coal mine in Dean Lane, the 1871 Census listing numerous working class occupations and a number of empty properties. The building alongside the car park is home to Carr Power Products, a busy power tool business. From the late 1930s, the building was occupied for over 50 years by Lenthall's, furniture manufacturers (**see 37-47**). There appears to be a history of furniture trading here, numbers 43 and 45 used by Thomas Darby, furniture dealer in the 1920s. As a child growing up on British Road, Bob

3-5 North Street 2014

Bennett remembers peering over at the rear of Lenthall's premises.

*They had a big carpentry shop at the back which backed onto the allotments owned by the church. I used to spend a lot of time there and I can remember looking over the wall into Lenthall's and on the other side of the wall was the Rex car park. This would have been in the late 40s, early 50s.They made good quality timber furniture and had a very big showroom.*

Frank Phillips also remembers the shop: 'They sold furniture, carpets etc. We bought our first dining suite there. I knew Vic Lenthall when I was an apprentice electrician. We thought they

1825 Bristol Directory

were rich because they had a TV and we used to go there and watch Harry Worth.'

George Carr and Sons took over the building in March 1985, having relocated from Lawson Street, Old Market where the business was established in 1858. Nowadays, Carr Power Products is owned and managed by Martin Jarvis and his son Luke.

Housed in another of North Street's historic buildings, the Hare (**see 51**) with its eye-catching sign is the first of five traditional pubs, each with an interesting history, along North Street.

Other shops which formerly operated along this section of North Street included a greengrocers (55) run for nearly 40 years by Arthur Saunders. Bob Bennett remembers Mr and Mrs Saunders in their green overalls: 'They were both quite dapper and would show me across the road to school [he attended Southville School]. I was about five years old then.'

**23**

The shop front c1937

# 9 HJ PITT, BAKERS

(NOW ELIZABETH'S PLACE)

**Joan Marsh (nee Payne) was born and grew up in 9 North Street, her family's bakery:**

*I was born in 1936 and my family came there in 1934 during the 'slump'. Originally it was my father's sister's [business]. She married Harry Pitt, but he dropped dead and my dad, John Arnold Payne, who was working on the vans delivering bread sort of took over without planning to do it. He found that the business was really on its edge and was given a month by the bank manager, and then it was stretched to three months and so on. By the time the Second World War came, business was picking up so Dad stayed put because he was in a reserved occupation. I don't know if that was the case with all shops but a lot of them seemed to stay the same during the War.*

The building which was used as the bake house is still at the back of the yard, through the arch. Joan remembers sheltering there during the Bristol Blitz, protected, so the family liked to believe, by the sacks of flour.

*There were steps where the men used to take the bags of flour up when it was delivered by Spillers. It would go up to the very top and when they wanted flour it would go down through the trap door. There were four coke-fired ovens and two furnaces that were kept going 24 hours a day. They started baking at 2.30am. Harold, who was the main baker for the dough, used to come in then and his helper would come in later. All the tins had to be greased and the dough put in to rise. I'm not sure what time the confectioners used to come in – about 6am I think. There were two and an assistant. The main confectioner made the cakes and Mr Barnes who lived in Hotwells used to do the icing on the wedding and Christmas cakes.*

These were the days of delivery by horse and cart, as Joan well remembers:

*Dad had two rounds, one over Redcatch [Road] and one in the Novers [Hill] area. The horse's name was Bob and the other horse was called Queenie. Bob knew the rounds and all the best dustbins! He was stabled at the top of the yard on the right hand side. When Dad sold the horse, he had to get a van because he couldn't get anyone to drive a horse. I think he went to a rag and bone man in Dean Lane. I was coming out of Blackburn's one day, looked up the road and there was Bob and his head came up and he started walking down towards me. If Dad did the rounds he'd take us with him and I used to love sitting up in the cart.*

As with other shop trades, local bakers were always willing to help each other out as Joan recalls: 'There were lots of small bakers in side streets in Southville and they'd often ring up because they'd run out of bread. My father would bake all the loaves and buns for one lady to sell in her shop.'

The early 1950s saw the advent of mass-produced sliced bread, as well as the expansion of larger bakers' companies, and Joan's father decided that enough was enough, eventually selling the business to Luton's (**see 226**).

Trevor and Joan Payne in the bakery yard of their home HJ Pitt, 9 North Street c1940

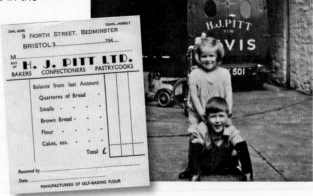

# 11-13 GARLANDS ZERO G CYCLES
(NOW EMPTY)

Staff at Garlands Zero G, prior to its closure. L to R: Matt, Tom, Damon, Josh

**Re-built after the Second World War, until recently this building was used as a cycle shop: firstly the independently-owned Garlands; and then around 2008, the Garlands Zero G company.** The latter company had four shops in Bristol: 'We've kept part of the name of the previous bike shop here, Garlands, as people still come to us looking for this name,' said Damon, a member of staff.

Damon thought the reputation, as well as the knowledge of staff who were all 'mad-keen cyclists', were its key selling points. 'We've got everything that could possibly be needed, a huge range, mountain bikes, road race bikes and we've got staff who are more than enough experienced – yes, we are all cyclists, big time.' 'A lot of the customers are local, but at the same time we get people from quite far afield, such as Scotland,' added Josh. There is a website, 'for bits and pieces, but for bikes it's largely the sort of thing that people want to come and collect. We show them how to do different things with the bike; we have a fitting station so we set people up on their bike to ride off.' Had the London 2012 Olympics boosted sales? 'I'd say no – nobody came in with a sign saying "I've watched Bradley Wiggins and I want to ride a bike!"' said Damon, 'but one would like to hope it has made a difference.'

Josh didn't see the presence of another bike shop in North Street as a problem: 'Relationships are fine. It's quite a small industry and we get on well.' His colleague Damon added:

*Our real rivals are, of course, web businesses. There used to be a time when we could also compete on price – but we can't anymore. Our business is not about capitalism but service, selling bikes and clothing. We are a customer-serving business, but that is both our strength and our Achilles Heel, because of the costs of employing staff. What's the point of being an expensive showroom for people only to buy them on the Net?*

Less than a year after this interview in 2012, the shop and company had closed – perhaps a victim of internet shopping.

# 19-25 THE REX CINEMA
(SITE CURRENTLY BEING REDEVELOPED)

**Jack House remembers the golden years of cinema-going in the 1940s and 50s, 'Queues of patrons extending right round the building, the commissionaire from time to time announcing in a loud voice that seats were available in different price ranges, 1/6d, 2/6d, 3/6d.** Having purchased the necessary tickets, you entered the cigarette smoke-filled auditorium and, with the assistance of the usherette's torches, were shown to vacant seats.'

Like most cinemas of the period, the programme at The Rex usually changed halfway through the week, resulting in plenty of variety. Once admission had been gained, patrons could stay as long as they wished and it was not uncommon for people to sit through two showings of the same film. Steve Williamson was a regular at The Rex during the late 1960s and early 70s: 'Whatever was on we watched it for 4/6d in the stalls. For £1 you could buy tickets and have an ice cream in the interval – two of you!'

High spot of the week for many children was the Saturday morning trip to the local cinema, the 'Saturday Rush', as Bob Bennett recalls:

*I was an 'ABC Minor'. On a Saturday it cost 6d. You had to queue outside, but if you went from British Road down Albert Place and climbed over a wall you could*

A new lease of life for the Rex cinema as Gala Bingo, a popular venue

An adult-only programme c1979

sneak in through the fire doors. The kids were always raucous – standing, shouting! Then the manager would come along, the film would be switched off and he told us if we didn't sit down and shut up the film would be finished.

As well as the trick of slipping in via the fire door, Frank Phillips recalls another well-practised childhood dodge:

*One would pay to go in and the other two would slip in at the side through the fire doors opened by the one already in there. They soon got wise to this and*

*they put an alarm on the door. We were all members of the ABC Minors and we'd sing 'We are the ABC minors, we pay our tanners, we know our manners'. They would ask if anyone had a birthday and one of us would go on stage. They'd ask your name, age when your birthday was – 'Oh... a couple of days ago' – and they'd give you a card with a pass which would allow you and a friend to come in free the following week. Everyone would sing 'Happy Birthday'. The next week when two of us got in free, another of*

*us would go up on stage and say it was their birthday and we'd get another two free passes and we'd take it in turns until they found out we were having them on!*

In order to help keep order, regular attenders like Doug Harris were appointed 'monitors':

*I remember that Lionel Hawkins was Senior Monitor and I was his deputy. All the monitors wore arm bands saying 'ABC Monitor' to show we were in charge. We had a secret that we were* told must not be passed on to any of the hundreds who turned up to watch the films. If the word 'fluke' was flashed onto the screen, it mean there was a fire in the cinema and the Monitors has to clear the place and would not allow any panic among the hundreds of little horrors who just wanted to see the film! Luckily it never happened, but we were prepared.

ABC Minors recall singing the National Anthem before the films began, the words of the Anthem appearing in white on the black screen with a little white 'ball' bouncing from word to word to help the singers. Once the Anthem was over, Doug Harris remembers the morning's programme always started with a Cowboys and Indians film, followed by a space serial, Jeanne Allen's favourite being *Flash Gordon*:

*The weekly serial was the high point of Saturday mornings at The Rex. Chucking of sweet papers and gobs of chewing gum preceded it. The kids were noisy and impatient once Woody Woodpecker had done his turn, replaced by a second-rate black and white 'B' film. It was the serial that everyone had come for, left at a cliff-hanger moment the previous week. Then the chucking stopped and cheers and yells were directed with ear-splitting excitement as Flash appeared, tights unblemished by the raging inferno as he rushed to save Dale!*

The Rex also supported a boys' football team, The Rex ABC Minors, and Doug Harris was a member:

*The team was managed by a Mr Llewellyn who worked at the cinema. The high spot of our 1944-45 season was to play on the Bristol City ground*

in a cup final against the Evening Post Golliwogs team. We lost 1:0 and after a super tea, we were all taken on stage at The Rex and introduced one by one to the Saturday evening audience. We were most embarrassed.

As children became too old to attend as ABC Minors, cinemas offered other attractions as Phil Elliot recalls: 'As we got older we'd try and get into the 'A' films; you had to be 16 and then of course they'd ask when were we born and we'd get chucked out.' Ken Summerill seems to have had better luck. 'We must have been mugs in those days. We used to put like a flat cap on when we were 14 to get into watch an 'X' film, and they believed us!' Sheila

Interior publicity photo, Rex cinema

c1961. Pop star Adam Faith plays one of a group of Englishmen who travel to Loch Ness to fake sightings of the monster. Script written by Terry Nation, creator of the Daleks

and Glyn Williams resorted to another trick: 'When we were 14 or 15, because we were under-age, we used to go up to people waiting outside, give them our money and ask to go in with them. We'd tail-coat a stranger and then say 'Cheerio – thanks for bringing me in!'

The Rex suffered the fate of numerous similar cinemas across the country, facing increasing competition from television and the advent of multi-screen cinema complexes, finally closing as a cinema in 1980. The building then operated as a Gala Bingo hall until 2008 when it was boarded up and finally demolished in 2014.

## 27-31 BARCAN WOODWARD, SOLICITORS

👉 **Now housing one business, the building started life as three separate premises.** In 1910, it appears as a beer retailer, Frank Bishop, trading as the Friendship. In 1921, Thomas Tabrett and Walter Henry Fisher were running an upholstery business from number 29. By 1930, the Fishers' business had expanded to include millinery run by Mrs Sarah Fisher. Bob Bennett, who grew up a short distance away in British Road, recalls going to this shop as a child in the late 1940s:

*There was a hat shop at the bottom of the entrance to the car park behind The Rex and I remember going there with my mum and grandmother. In the shop there was a large mirror at one end and a dressing table in the middle. There were ladies' hats on the table and*

Looking east to the fire at Lenthall's (35-37). Note the Shell garage next to the pink and cream Masonic Hotel

*everywhere you looked.*

For more than 40 years, number 27 housed a cobbler's shop, for many years run by Hyman Goldberg and later his son, Louis who were almost certainly descendents of Jewish refugees from the pogroms in the Russian Empire, the surname being common in Mile End, London. The last shoe repairer to work there was Martin Reiss whose customers recalled could 'work wonders with shoes which seemed beyond hope in his cramped shop with a distinctive, heady smell of leather, glue and polish.' Bob Bennett said: 'I can remember taking shoes there to be repaired. You'd go up some steps and it was very dark and he used to repair them in the shop, not out the back.'

During the 1930s, 29 North Street became what was popularly known as a 'Chinese laundry'. Initially called the Cah Kee, it later became the second shop of Wu and Bing who also operated at number 34. 'There were no Chinese takeaways then – it was all Chinese laundries' recalls Jeff Coleman.

*There was one a few doors above where I lived and my brother Reg often used to go there to do some ironing and help them out as they did men's shirts and collars. It was done by hand as people do today, but then they used gas flats [irons]. While my brother was there, an incident happened round about the King's Jubilee in 1935. The owner of the shop wanted to be patriotic and decorate the front with bunting. He hung a large Union Jack from the upstairs window –about the time that the BBC informed people that they were not hanging their flags the right way up – and Reg pointed out the owner's flag was upside down!*

In 1976, a firm of solicitors called Gerald Davey & Co. opened at number 31, extending their practice into number 29 in 1980, followed a few years later into offices above the shoe repairer's business in number 27. Barcan Woodward was established in 1992 by Richard Barcan and Giles Woodward and took over all three properties in the late 1990s when the shoe repair shop closed.

## 37-47 LENTHALL BROTHERS, FURNITURE MANUFACTURERS
(NOW CARR POWER PRODUCTS)

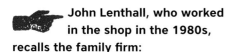 **John Lenthall, who worked in the shop in the 1980s, recalls the family firm:**

*I think my great grandfather started the business up. His name was Thomas Lenthall and the first shop was halfway up Redcliff Hill. My grandfather, Edward Lenthall, then ran it on his own until my father, Ted, took it over with Gilbert his brother. They went into partnership in 1946 and when Gilbert died my father ran it on his own. My brothers Victor and Philip worked there for a time. By then, the furniture-making had more or less ended and it was more re-upholstery. It died out because there was no-one really to take over. The family also ran another shop, 64 Stapleton Road, managed by my uncle, Tom Lenthall.*

Lenthall's was noted for selling a wide range of furniture, originally made in workshops behind the shop as John remembers:

*When I was young there was a house next door with an arch which you went through and that was where they used to make furniture. The upholstery workshop was also there and the frame makers were upstairs. When the big companies like G Plan came along the manufacturing died off a bit. I can remember the last three skilled workers: two were chair makers and one was an upholsterer who stayed with my father until he retired. His name was Lou Haberfield and he used to live in Gathorne Road. We were still upholstering because we had a big contract with Wills' who liked to use local businesses.*

In July 1973, the premises were severely damaged by a fire. 'Immediately after the fire father opened up part of the shop, put a chair and desk and people still came in to buy furniture. Me and my brother then rebuilt it,' recalls John Lenthall. Special permission was obtained to replace the original gabled roof with a flat one which gave a contemporary look to a much older building.

## 51 THE HARE

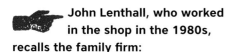 **The building next to the Hare (49), once a pub, is one of the oldest in North Street and of great architectural interest.** The rear section was built in the late seventeenth century with a wooden shop front added in the early to mid-nineteenth century. Although originally a dwelling, by 1720 the building is documented as the New Inn, much later becoming the Artichoke as listed in 1789. By 1874 the public house was known as the Full Moon, but soon afterwards (1883) it was in residential and commercial use after the public house itself had moved next door to number 51. In 1938 the rent paid by landlord Charles Williams, a tenant of Georges & Co. Ltd., was £40 per annum.

In 1864, the Artichoke was the focus of a crime allegedly committed by William Longbotham who was managing the pub for his brother, Frederick. Details of William's subsequent hearing before magistrates were described in 'The Bristol Mercury' on 23 July 1864, where it was revealed that he was found to be in possession of various items of silverware which had been stolen from Rev AH Ward and George Nash, ships' chandler and sail maker of Cumberland Road. When the property was searched, other items were recovered and William Longbotham sent for trial.

Following the closure of the Full Moon, the pub premises were refurbished and reopened as the Hare in March 2012. This free house is run by a manager, John Bunt assisted by Tom Bensted whose aim is to serve a selection of good quality drinks and locally-produced beers from the Box Steam Brewery and New Bristol Brewery. As John explained: 'We've had to work hard to attract a new clientele and the place is usually busy, even though unlike most pubs we don't offer food.'

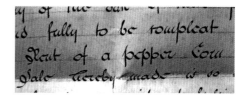

Number 49 is one of the oldest buildings in North Street. In 1793 the rent for the Artichoke public house was one peppercorn a year. Though a nominal amount, this ensured that there was a binding contract

# BRAUNTON ROAD TO HEBRON ROAD 57-65

Mike Beese poses for the camera outside his antiques shop, formerly Collard's, 2012

This section of North Street begins at Braunton Road, one of several side roads named after west country places (see also Dorset Street, Truro Road, Exeter Road, Dartmoor Street and Exmoor Street). On the corner of Braunton Road, which rises steeply from North Street, stands Michael's Antiques (57) run by Mike Beese. The tiling below the window looking onto Braunton Street displays the name AD Collard picked out in green lettering with a burgundy border. This, combined with the distinctive metal racks along the front of this property, provides clues of its former trade as a butcher's shop (**see 57**).

Next door is Rachel's Quality Second-hand Goods, occupying numbers 59-61. Rachel Dowding, the owner, is the daughter of Mike Beese and runs a thriving second-hand furniture business which opened in 2000. As Rachel explains: 'Although they are two separate businesses, I work closely with my father. He sells the high-end antiques and collectables while I deal with more popular items.'

For many years, from the 1920s to 1980s, number 61 was a fried fish shop which latterly traded from 59 as well which may indicate the popularity of the shop. Over the years, the business was run by Miss Jane Farrow (1920s); Alice Mines (1930s); Stanley Brunker (1930s and 40s); William Meen (1950s); and finally Keri Evans (1960s to the 1980s).

# 63-65 THE OLD BOOKSHOP

 **With its distinctive frontage, this café/bar opened in 2011 and expanded into the adjacent building (formerly Hibiscus, selling natural therapy products) in 2013.** Prior to this, number 63 traded under three different owners as a boot and shoe repairers from the 1920s to 1980s and later as a second-hand book shop where customers could also buy tea and coffee, hence the current name.

# 57 COLLARD'S, BUTCHERS
(NOW MICHAEL'S ANTIQUES)

Alfred Henry Collard and his assistant Ernest Harwood c1977. The straw boaters, striped aprons together with the most solicitous service, were hallmarks of Collard's in its heyday

**Collards began in the late eighteenth century with a butcher's shop in Temple Street run by Edward Collard.** His son opened a shop in Whitehouse Street, Bedminster where he had a slaughterhouse, while other sons Clifford and Charles ran butcher's shops in Old Market and Victoria Street respectively. Alfred's son, also named Alfred, married Florence Louise Melinda, daughter of another butcher (a Mr Woodall) and their wedding reception was held in the

Whitehouse Street slaughterhouse which had been scrupulously cleaned and freshly decorated for the special occasion! It was Florence, known as Louise, who came across the premises in North Street and persuaded her husband to buy it. By all accounts, she was a formidable person, running the business single-handed during the First World War and still working well into her eighties. In its hey-day in the middle of the last century, Collard's was a typical local butcher's shop with its name picked out in ceramic tiles, the interior fully tiled to create easily-cleaned surfaces, and a system of sturdy metal rails on which sides of meat were hung on display. As a child, Bob Bennett recalls 'the fresh meat hanging up outside Collard's.' For more information about the Collard family, builders and poets, **see 40**.

Brian Sleeman, whose father was another local butcher, remembers the Collard's shop well:

*One block down from our family butcher's was Henry Collard's shop. At that time, old Mr and Mrs Collard [Alfred Henry's parents] were still running the business. It was the tradition that all the butchers dressed their windows on the Sunday before Christmas – the old fashioned method where you put all your prime turkeys, chickens and pieces of beef in the window. Collard's was famous for it. You spent hours dressing the window, then you'd put on your best clothes and promenade down North Street, East Street and back up the other*

(Top) Alfred and Louise Collard with staff. Their delivery van dates this to the early 1920s. At the time it was customary to display meat outside, and the poultry show at Christmas was said to be especially magnificent. The brackets on which the birds are displayed are still there, and the assistant in the striped apron is probably holding the pole used to reach them. (Bottom Left) Still a butchers and bearing the Collard name, but no longer run by the family. c1996 (Bottom Right) Number 57, prior to renovation, 2013

*side looking at all the other butcher's shops and commenting upon how well they'd done. My father would cleave a carcass in half and if he didn't get it perfect he'd discard it and bring out another one. It had to be perfect because he knew that Henry Collard or Stan Butt or somebody else would look in the window and say 'You didn't*

*make a very good job of that!' Mrs Collard stayed in the shop until she was 100. She was always in the back, dressed in black, watching everything.*

Collard's continued until the 1980s, run by Alfred Collard (known as Henry), Louise's son. When he retired, the business transferred to new owners who kept the name Collard's.

# HEBRON ROAD TO
# MELVILLE TERRACE 67-81

Taken from the east end of North Street, looking west towards the Spotted Cow, which can be seen in the distance. On the left is Collard's butchers (57). On the right the corner shop with an awning (70) was pawnbroker Levy & Son, later to be replaced by the Somerset & Wilts Trustees Savings Bank. Nearest to the camera on the right is William Nash, tobacconist, selling Klondyke cigarettes, c1910-1921

**T**he bland exteriors of this short rank of buildings indicate little of earlier times when the shops here sold cooked meats, fruit and vegetables, bread, cakes and confectionery. In the early 1920s, Fraser Andrews, watchmaker, began business here in number 71, later moving further along the road (**see 235**). From the 1940s till the early 1970s number 69 was a bicycle shop

run by William Tucker. 'He sold bikes and repaired them – much like today but not as grand,' recalls Bob Bennett. For the first 30 years of the twentieth century, number 81 was the main post office for North Street, by 1930 offering a telephone service but pointing out to customers that 'telegrams are dispatched but not delivered.' The shop later became a butcher's, at one time run by the Sleeman family (**see 119**).

## 73-75 BRISTOL EAST RADIO
(NOW OFFICES)

Mark Manning, who worked in the North Street branch as a service engineer from 1978 to 1999 describes the family business:

*On their return from the [First World] War my grandfather, Clifford, and*

75 North Street, 2014

## WILLIAM GOULSTONE OF BEDMINSTER HOUSE

This is an etching from the prospectus issued by William Goulstone, senior churchwarden of St John's Church in 1840 and proprietor of Bedminster North Side Colliery.

The colliery, also known as Goldstone's Pit, was a short distance away at the junction with South Street. Mr Goulstone moved his Academy to Bedminster House in 1829. The prospectus offered 'Particular regard to the morals and gentlemanly conduct of the Pupils and every effort is made to develop their mental powers & improve their tempers and dispositions.'

Goulstone sold Bedminster House in the early 1860s and it was demolished in 1892.

The artist would have been standing near the current Club Cars taxi service (78). The raised pavement ran for a considerable distance along this side of North Street at the time. It has been said that the front doors of numbers 87 and 89, which now have flights of steps, were once level with this terrace.

his brother Charles formed Manning Brothers, Motorcycle Engineers in Melville Terrace. The shop in North Street was purchased by their father, Charles, in 1898 I think when the property was built on the site of a brewery [the Imperial]; he was a furniture dealer and cabinet maker. The brothers started by filling and charging accumulators and batteries. The business was then taken over by Bristol East Radio in 1926, Clifford becoming a director. Other directors were a Captain Bush [the same family which owned Bush House, home of the Arnolfini] Mr Vowles and Mr Featherstone. Bristol East Radio took over number 75, then purchased number 73 and before the Second World War its main business was the sale and rental of radios, radiograms and domestic appliances. There were branches in Knowle, St George, Old Market and 6&7, Lower Arcade in Broadmead where there was a recording studio with a grand piano. Anyone could turn up and cut

their own 78 disc. The Lower Arcade was destroyed in the Bristol Blitz. After the war the business went from strength to strength, increasing the number of television sales and rentals and opening record departments in each branch. The last manager of the North Street branch was Bill Ashman who lived in Ashton. The record department in this shop was especially busy on Friday afternoons as nearby Wills' factory finished at lunchtime and all the girls, desperate to get the latest '45', would head to the shop which used to be full to overflowing! The service department was in the Old Market shop with three bench engineers and three or four outside engineers. Unfortunately, Bristol East Radio failed to move with the times and couldn't compete with competitors who provided a similar service at a discount price. In later years we traded as J Manning Sales and Rentals, but my parents suffered from ill health and the decision was made to sell the shops.

# 77 SOUTH WESTERN TYPEWRITER SERVICES

(NOW EMPTY)

 **Jeff Johnston knows his Imperials from his Smith-Coronas, having spent much of his working life in the typewriter business.** Leaving school in the late 1950s, Jeff went into the family firm run by his mother's brother, 'Uncle Tom' and a business partner, Toby Phillips, and completed a five-year apprenticeship. The company started in 46 Alpha Road, Southville, working from a shop with accommodation above. After legalised betting shops were permitted in 1961, the shop was taken over by local bookmaker, Monty Maxfield, and the typewriter firm moved its workshop upstairs.

Jeff recalls life as an apprentice:

*When I started I always had to wear a studded collar and tie – even when I was behind the scenes washing the car down or sweeping the floor. Uncle Tom said you must wear a stiff collar: it cut your neck off! We all used to drink at the Imp. You'd go to a lock-in and half the Bedminster police force was there!*

The firm moved to 77 North Street around 1967. It was a furniture shop [Herbert Fryer's] when they moved in and Jeff recollects that 'it had a showroom downstairs, workshop and offices out the back and also had workshops upstairs.' The company name was South Western Typewriter Services, its headed paper bearing the strapline 'Service with technical skill'. The business flourished, due to commercial contracts, as Jeff recalls:

*We had contracts for servicing at Southmead Hospital and the same at the BRI [Bristol Royal Infirmary]. We did the work in situ: a couple of us would go round with our repair kit. Uncle Tom and Toby were very lucky. They picked up a very large contract at RAF Brize Norton. This was a lot of travelling for us, but it made a lot of money. Then we expanded and moved on to Greenham Common and Upper Heyford. Then we started working for all the American Air Force bases in the UK, servicing and overhaul. We didn't supply the typewriters as they all used Remington Rand, an American company. There was a senior engineer, Brian Flower, and myself. We used to stay in a 'B & B' and work on the base for a couple of days. At Greenham Common, I got caught in the Cuban thing: we were kept on the base for 72 hours. We also used to have a contract with Bristol Library. They used to have a machine that was a 'Noiseless' because it was a library. However we didn't do the Wills Factory as they had their own typewriter maintenance team. I used to look out for a job there – they were such good employers.*

Jeff remembers the old days. 'We used to have to send to London for parts and I'd go to the post office in Cannon Street to collect them.' As well as corporate customers, there were plenty of local people too:

*People brought in their typewriters and we would repair them, sell them, or recondition them. Sometimes they used to have really old machines, but Tony could deal with them because he'd been in the trade so long. I saw the beginning of the end of mechanical typewriters and when electronic typewriters came in we trained and worked on those too. We worked Saturdays and Sundays: if we were there repairing, then the shop door was open – people were always dropping in, buying ribbons and paper.*

With a travelling repair service, the company needed vehicles, and Jeff recalls that they 'bought our first vans from Bristol Motor Company [in Ashton Road].' His uncle's name was Frederick Herbert Thomas Williams, and 'one of the first vehicles my uncle got was a Morris 1000 van and its registration number was FHT 46D.' Jeff worked in the family firm until the mid to late-1970s, but then went to work for other typewriter firms. Apparently Tom and Toby 'tempted him back with an H reg Vauxhall Astra company estate car!' Eventually, though, as the partners got older, the business closed. Technological change brought about the total disappearance of businesses such as South Western Typewriter Services, their modern equivalent being computer repair shops (see 237 and 245).

# CHAPTER 4

# MELVILLE TERRACE
## TO SION ROAD 83-93

here are no longer any shops on this stretch of the road and several properties have been in residential use for many years. The building now occupying 91-93 was built on the site of the White Lion, destroyed by bombing during the Second World War.

## 83-85 ALFRED BEER AND SONS, LADDER MAKERS
(NOW OFFICES)

 'The ladder people where we went to for sawdust for our rabbits.' Ken Smith

In the 1860s and 70s, vast numbers of Scandinavian whitewood poles were imported via Bristol Docks to meet the demand for scaffolding, caused by the house-building boom. Steel scaffolding poles were not in use at the time. A familiar figure at the Docks may have been Joseph Beer, looking out for the perfect lengths of pole. Joseph Beer was a carpenter and wheelwright living in the village of Almondsbury, north of Bristol, and a family story suggests that he also made ladders from the spare spokes taken out of cartwheels that he repaired.

Joseph, his wife Amelia and their family moved from Almondsbury to 2 Perry Hill in Southville and established

Ladder poles on a horse-drawn dray outside Alfred Beer's factory in North Street. Sometimes it was necessary to stop the trams so that the very long loads could leave the yard. The main factory entrance is to the right (85), and on its left is the family home. The caption on the side of the load reads 'For Jerusalem Palestine.' Note the tram lines in the cobbles. c1932

the family ladder-making business there in 1869. Perry Hill was a country lane that led from the vicarage down to North Street. All three of Joseph's sons followed in his footsteps as ladder-makers, but only Alfred Beer's business survived. In the early 1900s, Alfred purchased 83 North Street, known as Albany House, for the family home, a few years later in 1905 purchasing the adjacent building (number 85) for the ladder-making business. As well

as the building trade, Alfred Beer and Sons supplied ladders to the Post Office telegraph service and fire service. During the First World War the firm was required to make ammunition boxes and between the wars they supplied thousands of long poles with wire cages on the end, to be erected as radio aerials on chimneys across the Bristol.

The ladder-making process started with the splitting and seasoning of the poles, done with a power circular saw,

35

Undated, but may have been taken at the Bristol International Exhibition, held nearby in 1914. Note the hanging photo, which is a similar pose to the other in this chapter, of the dray with ladders outside the ladder factory at number 83.

although traditionally this work had been carried out by hand. Over time, the company installed more machinery, powered by overhead pulleys and belts. A Crossley gas engine was lovingly restored by Alfred's brother-in-law Billy, who had lost his legs 'playing chicken' on the railway. Bernard Taylor started at the works aged 14, around 1922, with a job sweeping the wood shavings. In 1981 he was still there, aged 73, working as one of the four craftsmen.

The family, including Alfred's sons Ernest and Jack, continued to run the business at 83-85 North Street. However, around 1935 the former

Ashton Gate Brewery (**see 295**) had shut down and a relative of the family purchased the whole building, renting part of the yard to the family business on a 'peppercorn' arrangement. The firm moved there and prospered, with a great call for specialist fire-fighting ladders, as well as the traditional pole type. Another type of purpose-built ladder was manufactured for the General Post Office, used to erect telegraph poles.

During the Second World War the firm made ladders for the Civil Defence and Auxiliary Fire Service. Due to the pressure of running the business, Ernest suffered a nervous breakdown like his father, Alfred, had done in the First World War, so the firm was run by his brother Jack and Alfred's grand-daughter Kathleen.

Alfred's grandson, John Bradshaw, re-joined the company in 1947 after military service and took on sales and general oversight, as well as making ladders. About eight years later there was a slump in trade and then in 1968 the premises were flooded. Although the business had deteriorated, John and Kathleen were determined to build up the firm once more and the family pulled together. However, they had no stock of timber and so to keep the business going they expanded into aluminium ladders, flagpoles of wood and aluminium and, in John's words, 'anything they could make a profit from.' However, the rent had risen and with the lease due for renewal at the end of 1985, John and Kathleen decided to dispose of the business as a going concern after 120 years in the family. The new company did not succeed and the business closed not long after.

# 91 VALE VISION
(NOW EMPTY)

 **The business was run by Harold and Valerie Wood.**
Valerie explains how they operated.

*We'd previously run a shop called Raywood Radio because my husband was in a partnership with a Mr Reynolds. We moved into the shop in North Street in March 1960. In those days you had great difficulty in buying business property because you had to be in business for so many years in order to get a mortgage, so we were looking for somewhere to rent and we wanted living accommodation with it so we could provide a 24 hour service. When we moved into 91 the Gaywood House flats weren't there, it was a bomb site and it had a massive water tank in the middle which was used for putting out the fires during the war. Running the full length of our shop along Sion Road was a garden with an advertising hoarding and that was where The White Lion pub stood.*

*Our main business was repairing and servicing televisions and radios, as well as selling them. At one time we had the highest sales for Ferranti TV sets in the area. The government then decided to cut down on hire purchase. We had what was called non-recourse hire purchase, so if I sold a telly for £100 you'd pay £10 deposit and the finance company* would pay the balance. The downside was that if you didn't pay, we were liable to the finance company and would end up buying back the TV set for more money than we'd had off the finance company originally because of interest.

We lived on the premises and the shop was open until at least eight at night. We were one of the first companies in Bristol to have engineers with radio controls and at one time we had four engineers. If someone rang at ten at night we would try and get there. Bedminster was not a good area for receiving a television signal so a lot of people were on Rediffusion in those days.

When the first push-button TV sets came out we had a lot of trouble with them breaking down. Then Ferranti went into liquidation leaving us holding all the sets which we'd taken in for repair! Eventually they were taken over by Philips and their rep asked us if we wanted to carry on stocking new sets, but we said 'No we're going to go back to basics, servicing etc.' We carried on in that way from 1968, just my husband and I, until 1997.

We only repaired sets that were brought in to the shop. We used to close for August and people would come in during June and July to make sure they'd get their sets mended before we went away. Sometimes we had a chap called Mr Sandford who lived in the Chessels who would come and help us with the repairs, Mark

Harold Wood, owner/proprietor of Vale Vision and HG Wood & Son in his workshop c1984. The shop was the regional agent for ICOM ship-to-shore radios – hence the sign on the display

Manning of Bristol East Radio too.

Harold Wood and his son, David, were keen sailors and following a trip where they had to make do with a sub-standard ship-to-shore radio, they contacted a Japanese company called Icom. The outcome was the formation of a new company called HG Wood & Son who were agents for Icom. 'We supplied and fixed all the radios for the Harbour Master in Bristol as well as the coastguards from Portishead, Clevedon, Weston and Cornwall, and we did the fishing fleet out of Watchet and Ilfracombe. If anything went wrong with the ship to shore radio we would go and fix it, no matter where.'

As with other traders along North Street, Harold and Valerie had a good relationship with shopkeepers who sold similar products.

Bristol East Radio (73/75) were great friends. Also the Chiswells (78) who ran another radio and TV shop. Mr Chiswell would come over to us in the morning and we'd all have coffee. When he died his sons didn't want to know and his wife asked us if we wanted to buy it. We went and looked but it wanted so much doing to it so we said no.

We finished in 1997. My husband's sight was failing: he'd always had poor sight but he managed and was driving until he was 70.

Roy Gallop remembers Vale Vision from his sailing days: 'I bought my first Decca echo depth sounder [from there]. The owner was a guy who was interested in radio and radar, early installers of radio communications up at Bristol Airport.'

# SION ROAD TO DORSET STREET 93-117

(Left) View from the garden of Dorset House. The drawing is by William Curtis, from the scrapbook of resident CT Jefferies in 1857. (Right) Gaywood House block of flats, taken from the junction of Dorset Street and North Street. Constructed by Bristol Corporation (later Bristol City Council) in the early 1960s, the photo is likely to have been for the City Architects Department records

his stretch of North Street received a direct hit from a massive bomb during the Second World War. Numerous houses and shops were destroyed or badly damaged and several people killed. Dorset House, which had been the headquarters of the Bristol, West of England and South Wales Operatives' Trade and Provident Society until 1937, was also destroyed. Established in 1873, the Society was one of the earliest trade unions, offering support mainly to building labourers and dock workers. Its membership grew rapidly and when it opened its new office in Dorset House in 1898 it had 15,506 members, two years later becoming the second largest labourers' union. After the war, the area was cleared and the Gaywood House block of flats built as part of Bristol City Council's housing programme. Jantzen Derrick, who grew up in Pearl Street in the 1940s and whose uncle was one-time landlord of the Masonic (**see 110**), remembers the Dorset Street area well:

*Where the flats are [Gaywood House], that was all bombed and we had great fun playing on the bomb sites. Opposite, by the side of the Masonic, was all bomb sites up there as well. Dorset House was a boys' club – a youth club, but I didn't go there because I was a bit too young. The back of it was bombed but there was a shop at the front a florists called Barbara's.*

Before the War, the White Lion public house (93) stood on the corner of Sion Road, then a series of small shops,

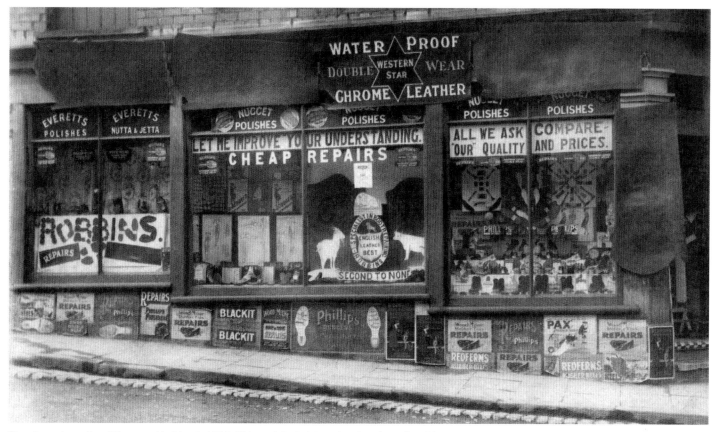

The shop at number 95 opened in March 1906. This undated picture is taken from the side, on the corner of Sion Road. The window display hints at the quirky style of Robbins, who was also a poet. The shop was gutted in the Good Friday 1941 air raid

including a boot repairer, wheelwright, plumber, butcher, milliner, confectioner , as well as the florist.

At the start of the twentieth century, John Robbins ran a cobbler's business in what was then number 95. Robbins' shop was one of several variously listed in street directories as boot and shoe makers, repairers or cobblers, which gives a clear indication of the importance of leather boots and shoes to the working class population of Bedminster. The Robbins family continued in business there until the Second World War.

The shops at the end of Dorset Street are recalled by Jim Nichols. 'On one corner of Dorset Street was Hills, the ironmonger's (117) where we could buy the paraffin and candles for lighting and charge up the accumulators [for wireless sets]. We would stand on this corner at Christmas to watch the decorated tramcar go by with Father Christmas waving from the open-top deck.'

John Robbins, cobbler, hand sewing a boot. John 'looked in now and again' at number 95 to give his son Gilbert Robbins a hand. John died c1910

# DORSET STREET TO SOUTH STREET 119-137

# CHAPTER 6

**"On the corner of Dorset Street was a butcher's which was a couple of shops along from William Maggs (123) who sold sweets, papers and was then a hairdresser's.** Close to this was a fruit shop where I remember having a halfpenny and buying half a pomegranate. Just imagine 480 half pomegranates for a pound – enough to give you the pip!' Jim Nichols

The butcher's shop referred to (119) was owned in the 1920s by the British and Argentine Meat Company, and then taken over by Alfred Sleeman. His son, Brian tells the story:

*My father, known to everyone as Fred, had a butcher's business at 119 North Street which had been there for quite a few years. It was bombed in the Good Friday blitz and I was evacuated to Coombe Martin. Apparently a land mine dropped in the centre of North Street and more or less destroyed everything. The shop on the opposite corner was Hill's which was a general purpose store and had tanks of paraffin and kindling which went up like nobody's business and was completely destroyed. The Dorset Street area suffered terrible damage in the blitz. A Scottish family by the name of Torrance didn't go into an air raid shelter and were in their living room when the bomb fell. They had a daughter, Rosemary and three sons, Donald, Brian and Alec. Rosemary was thrown onto the fire by the blast and*

Miss Mable Dunn outside her shop at 127 North Street, which she ran for around ten years from the mid-1920s

*suffered terrible burns. I can remember on that Easter Sunday my mother arriving unexpectedly to see us in Combe Martin. She then went on by bus to Ilfracombe where Brian Torrance was billeted to tell him that his parents had been killed and his sister was very badly burned.*

*We then moved down to premises on the corner of Melville Terrace, 81 North Street, which we occupied until about 1955. My father died in 1952 and the business carried on for a while with my mum running it. We had a*

shop assistant – Henry Taylor was his name, I think – and I helped too, but to be perfectly honest I wasn't cut out to be a butcher. I was 22 when my father died and had just finished my National Service. We ran the business for about three years after my father died before we decided to sell up.

The hairdresser's run by William Maggs is also remembered by an anonymous contributor .

*Having finished a three year apprenticeship I answered an advertisement in the Hairdressers' Journal asking for a gent's hairdresser in Bristol, 'live in', meaning board and lodging. The weekly wage was fifteen shillings, slightly better than my apprenticeship of five shillings the first year, seven and six the second year and ten shillings the third. I got the job in North Street, Bedminster at the Bristol City Barber Shop, owned by a Mrs Maggs. I'm doubtful whether there's anyone around who remembers the shop as it's well over sixty years ago. Mrs Maggs was a real live wire. She also ran a newspaper and sweet counter. Several of the Bristol City players used the barber shop: I recall Tot Walsh, May, Paul, Wedlock their average weekly wage was around three or four pounds, although in those day most of the players were on a part-time basis.*

*After the war, the premises were taken over by Bob Musselwhite ('A lot*

# 133-135 MOTORING DIRECT

 **Brian Parsons and Aaron Short set up Motoring Direct in November 2010.** They were both experienced in the motoring accessories business and decided to seek an opportunity to manage their own shop, looking at various streets before settling on North Street. As Brian explained, 'We had to find a shop that had a lot of local people and houses surrounding it, as well as a main road so that we'd get passing trade that way.' When they took over the shop, it had been empty for 18 months and was an empty shell which needed a lot of work to put right before the interior could be fitted out. Aaron did most of the work and has created a spacious, well laid out and smart shop.

Brian now runs the shop on his own and reckons that about 90% of customers live locally and those who come by car generally park outside the shop on double yellow lines, or find a space in a nearby side road. As part of the service offered by Motoring Direct, Brian is always willing to help customers by offering to fit parts purchased in the shop, 'anything within reason – wiper blades, bulbs, batteries, air filters, spark plugs, stereos. If it can be fitted on the side of the road, then I'll do it!' Most customers really appreciate this free of charge service and Brian is certain that quite a high percentage of people return to the shop because of this.

Brian Parsons, owner of Motoring Direct

'Many people come here because someone had recommended it to them and we're gradually getting customers from Bedminster Down and Knowle.'

Although he acknowledges the negative impact of Internet shopping on their business, Brian says the shop has done well since it opened and is pleased with the way that things are going.

News, booze and a 'Bedminster Bug', 2014

125 North Street, 2014

of people thought it was a mussel shop because of the name!' Joan Nurmeleht). Kevin Summerill worked there as a paper boy in the 1950s:

*I was only about 14 and had the best paper round you could dream of as it was so easy. I put one in Ronnie Dix's door, run across Myrtle Street and the three streets opposite and finished me round in five minutes! If anyone became ill I did their round and got paid 'double bubble'. There used to be a three star (Bristol) Evening Post – one in the morning, one in the afternoon and one in the evening. I did it Monday to Friday after school and I think I got seven and a tanner. Sometimes you'd be waiting in the shop for the papers to arrive,*

*the van would turn up and you'd sort the papers into the rounds. Customers would be on the 'phone saying 'Where's my Evening Post?' On Saturday I used to deliver the 'Green'un' and the 'Pink'un' sports papers as well and I think I got three bob for that. Then on Sunday morning I did a round, went home and back to bed for an hour, then went and collected money from customers and I got ten bob for that! I think I was Bob Musselwhite's highest-paid paper boy! The owners were lovely people. They had an adopted daughter called Cherry. You went into the shop and on the right hand side was the main counter. They sold cigarettes, newspapers, Airfix kits and a few toys, but not Dinky Toys which*

**41**

*you always got from specialist Dinky Toy shops. I worked there until I got a proper job. There were three of us paper boys and we all went to school together, Chris Gordon, Andy and me. Mr Musselwhite used to get frustrated with Andy who used to do the round along Smyth Road and could often be found sat on the kerb reading a comic, especially in summer. Bob Musselwhite was a very influential person with the Clifton St Vincent's Football Team and I believe there's a trophy in his name.*

Number 125, now Peter's Barber Shop, was at one time a children's clothing shop, run by Ronnie Dix. Dix had previously been a star player for Bristol Rovers, holding a regular place in the team from the age of 15 until ending his football career aged 34. He was widely regarded as very talented, transferring to Blackburn Rovers in 1932 for a fee of £3000. 'I'm sure the shop was his mother's, but he ran it in his name. He was fairly thick-set with a bald head' recalls Dave Russell, while Clive Green remembers that 'Mrs Dix used to get things knitted for babies and sell them in the shop.'

The bombing recalled by Brian Sleeman and Jantzen Derrick caused extensive damage to both sides of this section of North Street. Numbers 119-125 were rebuilt in post-war 'utilitarian' style. Numbers 127-135 – imposing three storey brick and render properties, the windows on the upper floors having substantial stone surrounds and lintels – indicate how this terrace would have originally looked.

**CHAPTER 7**

# SOUTH STREET TO AGATE STREET 139-163

**T**he narrowest stretch of North Street begins just beyond the junction with South Street, the last of four streets in Bedminster named after the cardinal point of the compass and prior to this, Northside Lane. The Spotted Cow (139) was serving beers, wines and spirits in the latter part of the nineteenth century, the landlord in the 1870s being James Wellstead and the pub perhaps so-named in order to attract farmers and their employees as they came and went along this route between the countryside and Bedminster, and the city of Bristol itself. The name of the pub is carved in capitals in the original stonework above the windows of the bar, alongside the name of the brewery which built and owned the pub, Georges & Co Ltd. Pale Ales, the company initials displayed above the corner entrance. At one time, three generations of the Tucker family lived in the little house attached to the Spotted Cow. George and Amelia Tucker raised seven children there and George's

The Spotted Cow. Ernest Parkman's undated watercolour portrays the street around the late 1800s. The building to the right of the inn was the St Francis Mission House, later replaced by the current pub entrance. The garden and trees were connected with the former Ashton Lodge

father had a part-time job as the 'chucker outer' at the pub.

From their current appearance numbers 147 to 153 seem to have been built as residential properties with front doors opening directly onto the pavement. They were, in fact, all in use as shops at various periods before reverting to houses. From the 1920s, the haulage firm of Charles Hawkins and Sons operated for more than 50 years from number 151 and a property on the opposite side of North Street (**see 204**) and their vans with 'Let Hawkins Do It' were a familiar sight around south Bristol.

Looking west from the junction with South Street. On the left is the hanging sign for George's Spotted Cow (139). The tram indicates that the photo was taken before the Second World War

## 157 FRED ROGERS, HAIRDRESSER

(NOW EMPTY)

 **The business was operating in 1910, the owner being James Rogers.** His son, Fred, took over the business shortly before the Second World War and continued until he retired sometime in the 1970s. Pat Derrick, whose aunt ran the shop next door, remembers Fred well, 'with his hair slicked back and a lighted cigarette always in his mouth, the ash hanging from the end.' Mike Rogers tells the story of his grandfather's shop:

It was my grandad's shop. His name was James, but he was known as Jimmy. My father was Frederick William and the customers called him Fred. We lived above the shop and I was born there in 1944. My grandad took bets from people. If you take off the wallpaper in the hallway you can see the bookie's board there!

It was very, very busy because Wills' was there and there was always a queue. The City players used to go there. The queue was outside the shop and all the shops were busy on their lunch break. On a Saturday he would cut kids' hair: he'd turn them away in the week and say come back on Saturday. It was six days a week.

My dad worked on his own. He didn't want to go into hairdressing so [at first] he worked for the Council. He opened at eight and he was busy right through the day. The shop was in the back of the house and the front was a sweet shop run by my mum, Violet Maud Rogers. If [someone] wanted a hair cut they'd walk through the sweet shop into the back. He had two chairs which were made in the USA.

Like his father and grandfather before him, Mike was also a hairdresser.

I started out working with my dad and then I went to a shop in Queens Road. I didn't have an apprenticeship I just watched my dad and picked things up. I used to sweep up the hair and pick it up and put it in the ashbin. Mum closed the sweet shop in later years [Mike thinks this was in the early 60s] and Dad moved to the front. Then they moved their living room downstairs. It wasn't a big house. It's still the same now, a hairdresser's with the same front door.

Mike thinks his father was in his seventies when he retired.

## 159 GILBERT WORGAN, FISHMONGER

(NOW RESIDENTIAL)

 At one time, the area boasted at least one shop

43

**selling freshly cooked shellfish.** Pat Derrick remembers this particular shop which was run by her grandmother, Violet Worgan:

*Their main line of business was cockles. They also sold mussels but only when there was an R in the month. Occasionally they sold winkles. The cockles were cooked fresh daily and my grandfather used to get up at about 5am to see to it. As well as doing this, he always had another job. The kitchen where the cockles were cooked was just a big, wet, stone floor. I can't ever remember them getting health inspectors in. The cockles came from Kings Lynn and Pembrokeshire on an overnight train and then by British Railways lorry from Temple Meads. They were in huge sacks and were bought in via an entrance leading from Agate Street.*

Dave Russell who worked as a van boy, operating from Temple Meads station, helped with the deliveries to Worgan's. 'I remember Vi Worgan. We'd have sacks full of cockles, dripping wet. We'd have a pair of sack trucks in the back and we'd sack-truck them in the back in Agate Street. Very often Mrs Wogan would give us some cockles. We'd deliver usually once a week sometimes one, sometimes two sacks.'

Once the cockles were cooked they had to be sieved to remove the shells; then they were put into large galvanised baths before being scooped up and taken into the shop in plastic bowls. The cockles were sold by the pint, half or quarter pint and measured out using small jugs.

*Quite often people would come with their own dishes or jugs because they wanted extra liquor and they'd ask for pepper and vinegar to be put on. I think they were 1/6d a pint. They would then be put in cellophane bags from the [nearby] Robinson factory. When the City were playing it was busy because people would call in and ask her to put back a pint of cockles and they would get them on the way home. She also sold Beavis lemonade in bottles which used to have the screw tops. People used to bring their bottles back because they get about 1d for each bottle. If they brought four bottles back they'd buy some cockles with the money.*

Rather surprisingly, given its main line of business, the shop also sold live fish as Pat Derrick recalls:

*They used to have a high counter made of metal and cut out in the front of the top part were two fish tanks with three more at the bottom with the goldfish in. On the customers' side my Nan had stands with tanks and behind the counter she had big stands with goldfish. She sold Fantails, Shabunkins, Golden Orf and terrapins – all along with the cockles!*

Lin and Kevin Cox remember going there 'as children to get our goldfish. They were about a shilling each.'

The nearest cockle shop at that time was Bryant's in Bedminster and Pat remembers how during the winter months when cockles were in short supply, the two shops would share their cockles so they could both keep going.

*My Grandad died in 1964 and my Nan carried on living there. A family friend, Chris Brown, took over cooking the cockles. My Nan died in 1980 when she was 80 and was still working in the shop until just before she died.*

## 161-163 WINDELL'S, GROCERS
(NOW RESIDENTIAL)

 **Vernon Windell was in Hull one day, browsing through books about trams.** He became quite emotional when he spotted a photo of North Street. It wasn't just the trams: Vernon could clearly see his grandfather's grocery shop, Windell's, where he had spent many Saturdays and war-time Christmases. The Windell family lived both at street level at number 161, to the left of the shop in North Street, and also above the shop at number 163. Vernon Windell recalls:

*The first floor room above the shop was the largest room in the house. I used to sit there, as a four year old, and watch the trams. This was the only room with windows onto the street. [My grandfather] used to keep all his stores and boxes in the yard out the back. At Christmas time we all went down there to Boxing Day lunch and tea, party games as well.*

Frederick's oldest daughter, Grace, was the only family member who worked there. She apparently 'married the errand boy,' as Vernon's story goes, 'who was somewhat younger than her. Grandfather owned the shop and she was just a paid servant in the shop.'

*Grace did all the weighing, but there were other shop-hands too, Marion O'Connor and Marion Oldfield. I remember as a very young child being given jobs by my aunt Grace. Later, when I got older, I used to pay into the Westminster Bank in Bedminster all his loose cash, my pockets weighed down with cash.*

Vernon has clear memories of his grandfather in this typical grocer's corner shop of the 1940s:

*There were marble tops where he cut his bacon and wrapped it in greaseproof paper. In this corridor at the back of the shop he would hang his pigs and then he'd cut off a piece and cut it up in the shop. They had safes with mesh to keep the flies out. I remember the very, very dangerous carving machine. I never went near that! Grampy was the only one who operated that, it was hand-turned.*

*I remember cutting up cheese and butter to put on the slab to sell. You had a square piece of paper and you folded it into a cone and screwed the bottom and put the sugar in. There were blue bags, they came flat with a folded bottom and you filled it and you put brown sugar in those. They had to be folded in a certain way.*

As you walked in there was a counter with tins of biscuits with glass lids. The cash register was by the door. The shop had bare wooden boards. They had old wooden chairs with the round backs, for people to sit on.

Vernon was a frequent visitor during the Second World War [he was

161-163 last traded as Able TV and Radio, here closed prior to conversion to housing

five at the outbreak] and afterwards:

*I remember when bacon was rationed and people could only have so much. [My grandfather] would get a certain amount each week. He was so scrupulously fair that he wouldn't supply anyone else unless he also had enough for his registered customers.*

Vernon recollects that:

*The shop closed early on Wednesday, opened on Saturday, but not of course, Sunday. He used to open at 7am to catch the Girls [the 'Wills' Girls'] on their way to work. He would stay open until 9pm on pay day because he knew the Girls would want to get their shopping on the way home. Much of the business they got from Wills and he would know when it*

*was bonus time and would get things like tinned lobster or tinned ham which the Girls couldn't afford at any other time, and he would stay open later.*

*He had a Christmas club where people saved with him. The people didn't just come in for their groceries, they came in to talk: it was a meeting place. He always had a grey overall coat on. I met people in my later time that had shopped in his shop in early years and they always thought he was a super man. If they had a harvest festival or Christmas celebration he would always give them a ham. There was no rivalry with other grocers.*

Vernon thinks his grandfather moved out in 1950. For a while the shop continued as a grocer, Silcock's.

**45**

# AGATE STREET TO THE NURSERY 165-185

Probably taken from the top deck of a tram, facing east, c1930s. Behind the waiting tram is the Spotted Cow, and adjacent is Vernon Windell's grandparents' corner shop, 161-163. Just in sight is Victor Tuckfield's tobacconists (171), now residential. Muriel and Ken Eley recall how they used to 'look for the workmen's return tickets so you could get on and have a free ride.'

gate Street is one of several streets in this vicinity which take their names from gemstones. Little evidence remains of the shops which operated along this stretch of road at various periods. A hardware shop, Waite's, stood on the corner of Agate Street and the same firm ran a builders' merchants and timber yard on the opposite side of North Street **(see 192)**. Diana Brown, who was brought up above the fish and shop (181) nearby, remembers how Mrs Waite and her daughter ran the shop. Kevin Cox and his sister Lin recall how they 'remember going up the steps to Waite's ironmongers and all the stuff

was laid out on different levels.'

From the 1920s till shortly after the War, number 179 was a hairdresser's run by Richard Ware, recalled by Ken Smith: 'Ware's the hairdresser, who had three barber shops [as] they did shaving as well as hair cutting in those days. They employed a young lad whose job was to sweep the hair off the floor and lather the customers. Then Mr Ware or his assistant would take over and shave the person with a cut-throat razor.' Mr Ware also ran a bicycle business in the shop next door (177).

Number 179 was last used as a catering supplies business which closed in 2013 when part of the building was

converted for residential use, but the original timber-framed, double-fronted shop window and glazed door have been left intact.

The row of three terraced houses, facing North Street at an angle with The Nursery, was formerly known as Albert Place, dating back to at least 1855. The aroma of fried fish coming from number 181 has been tempting passing customers since 1910 and from then until the Second World War it was run by Henry Wyatt, then for a decade by Harold Maggs until taken over by Dorothy Thompson **(see 181)**. For many years number 183, now the Beauty Lounge, was a greengrocers which made good use of the space in front of the shop to display goods. Number 185, once Hathway's grocers, is one of numerous hairdressing shops along North Street.

# 181 DOROTHY THOMPSON, FRIED FISH DEALER
(NOW ENID'S FISH AND CHIPS)

**Diana Brown is the daughter of Dorothy and Roy Thompson.** She was brought up above the shop referred to locally as 'Norah and Roy's', which sold both wet and fried fish, and recalls daily life and the hard work in the 1950s:

*We came from Devon. My grandad died young and my gran married again but decided she didn't want to stay in the village. Dad came out of the war in 1947 and my gran bought the fish and chip shop and also a house in Ashton Drive. I think it was hard for them because they'd never been in business. We lived over the shop, two bedrooms and one small room, and the kitchen was part of the outside yard. Because everything was so small, the stairs were*

Diana's father Roy Thompson cleaning the shop windows of his fish and chip shop at number 181. In the background is Luckwell House (201)

*wooden and weighted so they had to be pushed up, like a loft ladder.*

*Mum and Dad ran the shop and the person that they bought it from helped them for a while. There was a place in one corner on the left hand side where the wet fish was. Mum would sell the wet fish in the morning and afternoon and then they'd do dinner times and evening. Night times were busy when people came out of the pub. As it went on they had to sell more things like tinned fruit and soup and bottles of lemonade. They were open from 8.30am until 1.30pm, then have three quarters of an hour for dinner and Mum would be in the shop in the afternoon. Then they'd have two hours off and they were open again at 7.30pm until 11pm. They didn't open on Mondays. Dad would go to the market on Monday to pay the bill and Sunday they'd clean the shop right through.*

*Dad used to ring the order for the fish at night and it would be delivered in the morning. It would be left outside. You went out through the passage to what we called the fish house which was tiled and Dad would prepare the fish and the batter. We had a great big bath where Dad would put the potatoes to clean them and then [he] would stand out there every afternoon taking all the eyes out. The fish would come in boxes and Dad would break them up and give it to people for firewood. We used to have a lady come in and take all the fish heads to the Cut [River Avon] and feed the rats!*

Although there were several other fish shops in North Street at the time, Diana recalls that 'there was no rivalry between the fish shops. We would all

Diana Brown and her cousin Robin in her garden at number 181 North Street

help each other.' Diana remembers: *Match days were very busy. The queues could be right up around the Nursery.*

*[On] Good Friday they had to be up early because they had over 100 orders for wet fish. We sold cod and hake. We sold pies and I think they got them from Bowyer's at first and then from Clark's. The people would ask for plaice either done in flour or breadcrumbs.*

'Norah and Roy's' was succeeded by Enid's and local residents Linda and Ivan Carter, who lived nearby above the Home & Colonial shop (number 224) recall how 'on a Friday we used to go to the Hen and Chicken and have a drink, then go to Enid's and have fish and chips.' This would have been just after Diana's parents retired in 1973.

**47**

# NORTH STREET GREEN 187-199

**T**his is another section of North Street which suffered substantial bomb damage during the Second World War. Maps of the early part of the twentieth century show a row of small cottages on this site, destroyed in the same air raid which caused severe damage to the Hen and Chicken (**see 210-218**) and a large house on the opposite corner of Luckwell Road. Although there have never been shops here, the area deserves a brief mention. Ben Barker, a well-known community activist and champion of the North Street revival, explains:

*'North Street Green' is a recent development – a community project aimed at making best use of what was an area of untidy wasteland, now grassed and planted with trees and*

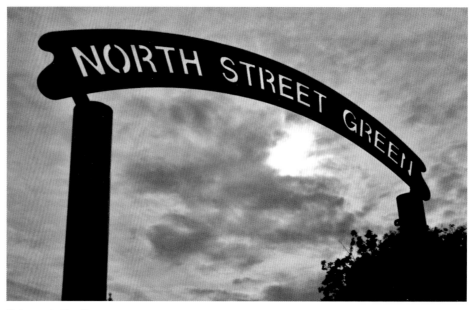

Gateway to the Green

*shrubs with seats to encourage people to stop and enjoy the area. The Green is* *used several times during the year as a venue for local events.'*

# LUCKWELL ROAD TO BALFOUR ROAD 201-207

**T**wo large buildings now occupy this site, an older stucco-fronted house linked to a modern Victorian-style villa, both now used as specialist residential accommodation. The older building has been modified from the original Luckwell House, which was built c1830-1850. For many years, this was used as the WD & HO Wills Evening Club, the names of various club stewards being listed in the pre-war street directories. Referred to locally as 'The Wills' Club' it seems to have been run primarily for the benefit of male employees who were aspiring to supervisory or managerial positions in the nearby cigarette factories.

# BALFOUR ROAD TO TRURO ROAD 209-215

From Balfour Road, possibly named after AJ Balfour MP, North Street gradually descends for a third of a mile until it meets Ashton Road. This is the widest section, creating an overall sense of space and light.

Number 209 started life in 1910 as a shop, a 'gas oven showroom' run by George Gay, presumably to meet the demand for the latest kitchen appliances which were gradually replacing coal stoves. Ten years later, the shop was owned by Paxman's Ltd, a well-known Bristol company specialising in dyeing and cleaning, and operated as 'a receiving depot' where items would be deposited and then dispatched to the Paxman's factory in St Werburghs. By the late 1960s, the business had changed hands, becoming the National Sunlight Laundries Ltd, cleaners and dyers. In the 1980s and 90s it was a

(Top) Taken c1905 near the current bookmaker (211-213), looking towards the yet-to-be-built tobacco factories, which later obscured the elaborate turret seen here on Ashton Gate School. On the right is Luton's Greville Steam Bakery (226) and Miss Pope's stationers (228). On the left is Truro Road (nowadays a bank stands on this corner)

(Bottom) Taken from almost the same place as the view above, the Franklyn Davey tobacco factory has now been built, as has the final rank of shops on the left

music shop with various electric keyboards on display in the window. Following this, the premises enjoyed a brief spell as the Green Bean Café. It is currently a 'budget booze' shop.

Corals, bookmakers, occupy numbers 211 and 213. Before and for a short time after the Second World War, the shops were in use as a greengrocers and butchers, originally owned by Alexander Tanner. Tanner's started life before the war in number 213, taking over the adjacent premises when Mrs Jessie Toogood ceased trading as a furniture dealer. Latterly, the butcher's shop was run by F Abraham and the greengrocers by Iles and Viney, although a bookmaker, WG Tanner, also operated from 211.

Andrews Estate Agents are at number 215 on the corner of Truro Road. From the 1920s until after the war, these large premises were home to David Levy and Sons, variously described as 'furniture dealers' or 'pawnbrokers' as Phyllis Neale recalls: 'There was a furniture shop called 'Dicky' Levy and at the back of his shop he had a pawn shop. He used to stand out on his door very well dressed, I knew him personally because I bought a lot of furniture from him when I got married.' From the 1950s the furniture business continued, trading as Small and Son Ltd, later known as Small's Furnishings – 'contemporary furniture and carpet specialists'. By the late 1960s it had changed its name to Briton's Furnishers Ltd. and its final incarnation was as a carpet retailer, Bailey's Stores (Bristol) Ltd.

# CHAPTER 12
# TRURO ROAD TO RALEIGH ROAD
# 217-275

**T**he junction with Truro Road marks the start of the longest rank of shops in North Street. This was the last substantial section of the street to be built and, as can be seen from the original builder's plan, the proposal was for a mixed development of five shops fronting the pavement, the remainder being domestic properties set back. In fact the eventual terrace of houses consisted of only eight buildings, all but one of these (number 239) now being a shop. The rest of the buildings in this row were constructed as shops, so prospects for the retail trade were obviously bright in 1904, presumably because of the completion of the terraced streets in Ashton and Southville. In the main, the upper two storeys of the whole row of shops have been little altered since being built – rag stone facing and sandstone window surrounds with gabled ends to the roofs. The western end of the row abutted the Ashton Cinema, built about ten years later in 1914, although another plan dated 1903 for this corner shows a public house – *The Sir Walter Raleigh*, to be run by the nearby Ashton Brewery.

A bank, originally a branch of the Midland Bank and currently the HSBC, has stood on the corner of Truro Road since the 1930s. Prior to this, the building housed a dairy run by Ernest Edwards and later his wife, Jane, in

the days of home deliveries by horse and cart, milk being ladled directly from churns into the customers' own receptacles. Complaints about finding horse hairs in the milk were common! The shop next door (219) has been in continuous use as an ironmonger's since just after the First World War (**see 219**).

Number 221, currently unoccupied, was last in use as a sandwich bar, the Flying Frog, run by a convivial Frenchman, Jean-Marc, who would stand in the doorway greeting passers-by. Prior to this, the shop had served as a drapers, Brett and Co; then from the 1950s it was occupied by Carlton Perry Gowns, the main window cleverly angled to reduce reflections and therefore allow 'window shoppers' the best view of the goods on display. Before the Second World War, the same shop had been Bessant's, confectioners (**see 221**).

Madras Express (223) is run by Al Bandali and specialises in Indian food cooked using family recipes. The restaurant opened in 2005 and was originally called Al's Hot 'n' Spicy but was forced to change its name due to customer confusion with its sister restaurant, the legendary Al's Tikka Grill on Ashton Road. In the early part of the twentieth century, the shop sold wet fish and was run by Eli Bence and in the 1950s and early 60s it was Blake's Medical Stores, selling intriguingly-

Photo taken c1920s near what is currently The Lounge (231). On the right at the corner of Gathorne Street is Mrs Mabel Hayman's fruit shop (252, now Parsons Bakery) and Arthur Lye's butcher (250, still operating as a butcher, Rare Meats). Just showing is Hedley Price (238), offering a 'Same Day Film Service.' Note the 'ghost' figures on the left, due to the long exposure

named 'surgical goods'. By 1968, the shop had changed to a branch of the well-known Bristol bakery, Mountstevens (**see 223**).

Still in use as a hairdresser's, Crowning Glorie (225) was for many years a barber's shop run by Frederick Coole. Mervyn Southway had his hair cut there when he was a boy and recalls a story about his uncle Len ('Lemmo') Southway who was a trainer for Bristol City Football Club:

*Fred Coole used to get loads of people. I think a haircut was 3d or 6d.*

*He did a lot of business, but you always had to wait because he was the only one there. I remember Lemmo used to take any new footballers that came to the City ground in there. There was one he took in to have a shave. He gave Fred the wink and of course he knew what it meant. He put on the lather then he got the cut throat razor and very hot water and started to shave the footballer. The footballer jumped up and shouted 'He cut me throat!' and he ran down the road.*

Numbers 227-231 are home to

The Lounge. This popular venue was established in 2002 by Jake Bishop, Alex Reilly and Dave Reid. Having spent a number of years in the catering trade in Bristol, the three friends decided to set up their own business, a small bar run by Dave, where they could meet friends for a drink. An empty shop (number 227) on North Street turned out to be the right size and already had a kitchen area at the back. Although initially there were no plans to serve food, it was soon clear that customers wanted to eat as well as drink and so

The tobacco factory dominates the view along North Street at its west end. The present day entrance is recent, where the window and blind is in this undated photo. On the left is Charles Treleaven's piano shop (269), which by 1930 had become a greengrocers. Next door is the Raleigh Road Post Office, which traded here into the twenty-first century, then a further shop and the Ashton Cinema

the three owners set about creating a simple menu. Such is the success of The Lounge that it has expanded into the adjacent two properties. The place is always busy, customers attracted by the informal bistro atmosphere, a place to meet, relax, eat and drink or sit with friends and play a board game over a cup of coffee or glass of wine or beer. 'Loungers', the company formed by Jake, Alex and Dave, has not only opened several Lounge venues elsewhere in Bristol , but also in other towns across the country and aims to open a further 15 'Lounges' by the end

of 2014.

For 50 years from the 1940s, the same three premises were occupied by the original branch of the Keith Pople chain of outfitters (**see 227-231**). Later, number 231 was Pete's Tackle Shop in the 1960s, 'selling everything a fisherman could want – rods, lines, maggots' says Pete Neale. The owner, Pete Wilson, was the son of Cyril Wilson who ran a pet food shop at number 254.

The Beauty Room, another of North Street's many 'beauty parlours' has been in number 233 for seven years and is run by Cleo Coleas-Canham, who

explains 'I was originally based in the David Lloyd Centre, then moved here and brought a lot of my customers with me. They love the location as they can do their shopping once they have had their treatment here.'

Now in her nineties, Phyllis Neale clearly remembers the watchmaker's shop next door (**see 235**). The name picked out in black and white tiles on the doorstep of number 237 shows that this shop was once a branch of Bollom Ltd, dyers and cleaners, founded by the Bollom brothers of Philip Street, Bedminster. It is now in use as one of two specialist computer repairs and sales shops in close proximity and is managed by Darren Baker. Beyond the last remaining house in this rank (239), is another hairdressers, You.

Number 243 is currently a branch of Connell's, Estate Agents and was formerly an off-licence, part of the national Threshers chain. Killed off in the main by the availability of cheap alcohol in supermarkets, off-licences have been replaced by 'budget booze' shops of which there are several along the length of North Street.

Number 245 is now the home of Personic Computers, but for many years was The Dinkie, another of North Street's much-loved shops (**see 245**)

247-249 AV Bristol, a specialist audio and television shop, opened in 2011 and is run by Jim Emsley and his son Jake. Jim set the business up in 2000, originally only selling goods via a website, but since the shop opened the trend is for more purchases to be made 'in store' where customers can both see and hear a range of equipment and benefit from expert advice. The shop had been in similar use for several years prior to this, its distinctive blue name board advertising Panasonic televisions and other products. Alma Chalmers still remembers the draper's shop (247) run by Mrs Emily Batten: 'A friend of mine had an aunt who was born in 1900 and worked in Batten's. Her name was Catherine Campbell and she said the staff had to go in very early. They were then inspected: they had to wash their hands and they had to be inspected afterwards to be sure their hands were thoroughly washed, their shoes were clean and their clothes were also

cleaned before they were allowed on the counter. She seems to think she started there from school which would have been during the First World War.' Phyllis Neale remembers the Battens running two shops, 'one for ladies and one for babies.'

Grenville Wick, cards and gifts, in number 253 is an off-shoot of the highly successful Southville Deli, run by Paul Wick. From the late 1930s through till the 1970s the shop was in use as a butchers, run by Norman Bennett. Next door (255) is a branch of Betfred, bookmakers. For many years, the shop housed hairdressers Kathleen's, and later, Jefferies. Alma Chalmers remembers going there with her mother: 'From what I can remember you had a machine perm in those days. You were wired up to this machine which frightened the life out of me, it looked lethal! You were all in cubicles with curtains around to separate you; it was very private. I remember my mother having it done – I would have been about 10, just after the War.'

Number 257, currently a takeaway pizza shop, Pimms Pizza, was formerly the Regency Café and before that, Barry's Café.

Number 259, Clark's Pies, is one of North Street's iconic shops (**see 259**). Glass Designs next door (261), which always has a window full of eye-catching wonders, has played a key role in the revival and stability of North Street as a place where independent retailers can flourish. Run by Claire Dadswell, it opened in 2003 in the former Allen and Harris Estate Agents office. The shop specialises in stained glass work, including lampshades and other glass

products including 'Bristol Blue', as well as selling a wide range of craft items and gifts made in or around Bristol. As Claire explained, 'When customers find just what they want they often say "It's brill – you've saved me going into town!"'

Number 263, Dimsum, oriental 'takeaway', for many years was Mills and Mills, chemists, much-loved by local residents.

Number 265, Clifton Beauty Centre, was previously the home of Paynter's Ltd, a paint and wallpaper dealer, run by Phil and Minnie Chappell. 'They offered a unique service – trimming

EB Edwards of Park Dairy, 217 North Street, orders nine gallons of cider from William Allen of Bradley House near Bridgwater. The order is dated July 1917. Cider is still produced at West Bradley, under the brand name 'Orchard Pig'

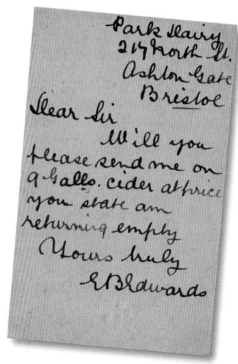

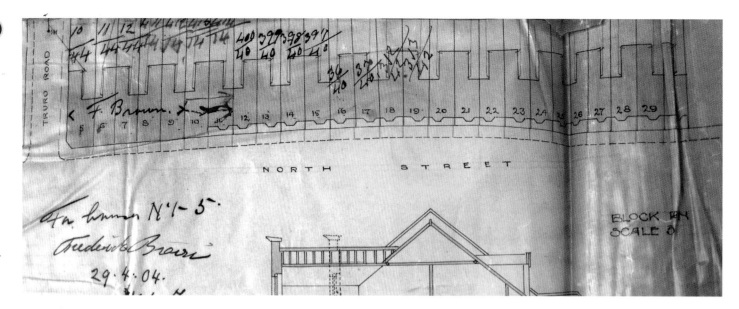

The 1904 building plans for the last section of North Street to be constructed. The right-hand end of the row was abutted by the Ashton Cinema about ten years later

the rolls of wallpaper with a machine developed by Phil Chappell. Otherwise it was the arduous task of cutting off the edge with scissors!' recalls Lew Pedlar. Steve Williamson also remembers watching, fascinated, while 'old Mr Chappell trimmed the paper on a machine which held the rolls.' Kevin and Lin Cox recall a fire breaking out, 'sometime in the late 1950s, early 1960s. [We] think it was an electrical fire. Apparently they lowered a lady through the ceiling over the back of the garage to get her out. I believe it was Brian Chappell's mother.' According to Pete Neale who, like Lew Pedlar went to school with Brian Chappell, Mrs Chappell senior then tried to walk across the flimsy roof and promptly fell through onto a new Ford Classic car underneath! Local traders rallied round to help, Gino from his cafe a few doors away, 'brought a tray of tea for the firemen.' (Pete Neale)

Fishminster (267) is the latest in a long line of fish shops occupying these premises, starting with Alfred Webber who changed his 'refreshment house' into a shop selling fish and chips sometime in the 1930s. The shop was taken on later that decade by Gerald Dollery, recalled by many older people including Rex Whitlow: 'We must have had chips from Dollery's nearly every day of the week – except Sundays of course. David Dollery played rugby, I think. He was older than me but I think I may have played against him once or twice after I'd left school. I think he was a number 9, but I can't remember for which club.'

Number 269, now Ashton Fruit Shop, has been in continuous use as a greengrocers' shop from the 1930s to the present day (**see 269**). Number 271 houses Northwood Estate Agents. From the 1920s until its closure at the start of the twenty first century, this building was home to the Raleigh Road Town sub-Post Office, run for many years by the Whitrow family who operated other post offices in the Bedminster area for nearly 30 years. The local post office now operates in the rear of McColl's on the opposite side of the road.

Savana (273) was, for over 60 years, a confectioners shop (latterly Yates) as Phyllis Neale recalls: 'There was a sweet shop next to the Ashton Cinema and by the side of it was a staircase up to a dentist. [He was a] great big man – they called him "the butcher"!'

Number 275, Ocean Estate Agents. This prominent corner premises was once the Ashton Cinema (**see 275**). The Ocean chain, with branches throughout Bristol and other cities, was established in 1983 and relocated its Ashton office here when the entire building was extensively renovated in 2008.

# 219 LION STORES

👉 **This popular shop, which has achieved something of an iconic status as one of the few independent ironmongers left in Bristol, is run by Derek Knapman.** Derek thinks that the original Lion Stores was founded in 1897 in East Street, Bedminster, in those days run by Moses Rennolds (sic) who later relocated to a premises in Warden Road. Round about the same time (Derek thinks this was in the 1930s or 40s) Moses Rennolds acquired 219 North Street which was then run by his wife, Topsy. Derek takes up the story:

*It's always been known as Lion Stores but we don't know why. When my dad left the army, he did various jobs including going into business with his father [as] Knapman & Son, builders who helped build the Southmead estate. I was born just down the road [in North Street]. My Mum worked in the clothes shop next door [221 Carlton Perry Gowns] and that's how she found out this shop was up for sale and mentioned it to my Dad. Various people looked to buy but eventually my Dad got it.*

*We've always sold ironmongery – nails, screws, washing lines, posts, wire, ropes – but if we were just doing that now we would have been out of business. You have to try and stay in tune with what's going on in your area so we've had to cut back on a lot. If a customer came in and asked for something which we didn't have we would get it for them. We expanded by going into gardening and plumbing and I did some night school courses on electrical. I did the same on the plumbing so when a customer comes in and asks how to do something I can pass it on to them.*

*We used to sell lots of models of shire horses and my dad and I used to go to Stoke [on Trent] to get them. This was in the 70s, then in the 80s it was better quality tea sets. We'd buy separate plates, cups and saucers and do them up in a 'poly-bag' as a set. We hardly sell any glassware, cutlery or chinaware now. It's hard to say what our biggest seller is. We used to have a very good paraffin business. When we were out of paraffin we used to have all the cans lined up with people's names on them waiting for the delivery to come in. They'd run the pipe through the front door and into the tank and as it was filling up we would be filling the customers' cans. We used to have 500 gallons at a time and when it was really in demand we would have two deliveries a week. Now we just buy in pre-packed, mainly for greenhouse heaters.*

Derek realises that shopping habits have changed over the years and this has impacted on the way shops like Lion Stores have to operate:

*We really feel the impact of big stores. Large companies get offered bulk deals from wholesalers – we*

Derek Knapman, proud owner of Lion Stores (219), displaying a Bristol Pound

*don't get that being a small business. It's hard to keep on top of it especially in the present climate. Business has slipped away really. When Cashsave (166-174) closed it didn't put £100 extra on my turnover. They would send people down to me and I would send people up to them and there wasn't any bad feeling. I didn't look upon them as competition as we always worked together.*

The spirit of mutual support and co-operation between the shopkeepers along North Street is promoted by the North Street Traders' Association of which Derek Knapman is a leading member.

# 221 BESSANT'S, CONFECTIONERS
(EMPTY AND UNDERGOING RENOVATION)

 **Jeane Johns describes the sweetshop run by her family in the 1930s:**

*I was born in North Street, Bedminster which 'toffee nosed' people referred to as Ashton. My maternal grandparents, John and Mary Bessant owned a sweet shop there. Grandfather was a confectioner and manufactured over 40 different varieties of sweets, candies and toffee. We were a close and secure family and just before the death of Grandfather Bessant and the beginning of the war in 1939 we moved to 21 Nelson Parade, next door but one to the Bedminster Police Station, and my parents carried on the confectionery business there.*

The start of it all was when Jeane's grandmother made sweets in her kitchen and sold them to children passing by on their way to and from school.

*My grandfather used her recipes as a base and soon improved his skills. I understood that by the beginning of the 1914 war he owned three shops and a workshop near the London Inn where all the sweets were manufactured. He employed several people. As my mother and her four sisters grew older they were not allowed to take up a career but expected to either help grandmother in the house, or grandfather in one of the shops. However, they had a good life and plenty of pocket money. I always thought that my mother resented the fact that she was not free and was expected to leave school at 14.*

Inside Mountstevens (223) the manageress serves two young customers with hot drinks in 'Lily carry cups'. Sausage rolls are ready for sale, under the slogan 'Local making – Fresh baking'

# 223 MOUNTSTEVENS, BAKERS
(NOW MADRAS EXPRESS, INDIAN RESTAURANT)

 **Mountstevens, a familiar name on high streets across Bristol, ceased trading in 2004.** Sue Mountstevens, the fifth generation of the family to work for the company, tells the story:

*The bakery business was started up by Henry and Ada Mountstevens, before 1911 I think, in St Mark's Road, Easton, making bread and cakes and selling it out of the window. My dad, Gerald, took over the bakery when he was 21. He'd never wanted to be a baker as he was a keen motorbike rider and he'd just been offered the chance to be a 'works rider' for AJS [well-known firm of British motorbike manufacturers]. When you're 21 this is the stuff dreams are made of, but then his dad died and he had me, my sister and his younger brother to look after, so he had to take over the family business.*

*My dad then went to bakery college, but failed his bakery exams would you believe! As we expanded we took over some businesses that were failing and that's why we ended up with a number of shops that were close together. North Street was absolutely thriving in those days. When you went to your local bakers you didn't venture far afield. We knew everybody and we knew what they* were coming in for whether it was a particular loaf or a Russian slice.

As a child, 'before Health & Safety', Sue had helped out in the shops: 'When your Mum's working in the shop and your Dad's there too, that's what you did. I can remember helping in the shop on Good Friday morning and every Saturday. I would go in and play in the office on one of those comptometers'. Later on, Sue went to work for her father having 'finished being a student and short of money.' She spent the following seven years in the bakery and was then 'allowed out into the shops.' Every shop had its own manager and the employees had to get to work really early, ahead of the delivery of fresh bread and cakes.

*My Dad insisted we had a full window display by the time we opened at 8am. No-one would walk past an open shop door as far as my dad was concerned so he insisted the door was left open from the moment we arrived at 6.30 or 7am every single day, six days a week – and we would freeze! We used to carry an incredible amount of stock: in the North Street shop we would sell something like 100 jam doughnuts every day.*

Sue recalls all the shop managers being female in those days.

*We made wedding cakes, birthday cakes and novelty cakes. I remember we had to do one for Clifton College in the shape of their chapel with its copper-colour roof – it took ages. There were several times when we did cakes in bits and we'd put them together in situ. We made all the wedding cakes for the Queen's Silver Jubilee in 1977. There was a big event at Bristol Cathedral and everyone who had the same anniversary as the Queen was asked to attend. We made wedding cakes for all of them and a lot of them said they'd never had a wedding cake (because of war-time rationing).*

In common with many businesses in the 1960s and 70s, Mountstevens provided a home delivery service:

*We had 15 or 20 guys who would go round to 'Mr Joe Bloggs' and deliver one small loaf every other day and we would have to go back on Saturday and ask the customers to pay up. We made so many lines, always stuff that Dad and myself liked. Every year we'd say we must cut some lines but we felt we never could. We might have only made 25 or so of a particular item a day, or even a week, but we knew people who would like to buy those so we continued to make these small lines in case we lost a customer.*

Mountstevens was famous for its 'Congo bun.' 'I remember that we were the only bakers in the whole of England who made Congo buns, the reason was that everyone else called them 'Belgium buns' but my dad couldn't spell Belgium!

As well as Mountstevens, the 1972 street directory lists seven bakers' shops along North Street: Sylvita Confections (9), Blake's Bakeries Ltd (74), H Baker (154), Ernest Jordan and Sons (156), Luton and Sons Ltd (226), and Zohrer (292). Like other trades people along the street, business was conducted in a spirit of co-operation.

*Luton's was not a rival. We were always good friends. Everyone would run out of yeast, mainly on a Friday night. You'd get a knock on the door, probably someone from Luton's, asking if we had spare yeast and we would lend it to them. We sold the business in 1997/98.*

There were a number of reasons: my Dad wasn't well and supermarkets were taking over the high street and the high street was reducing in size and it was becoming more and more that people were doing one big shop. It became clear if we were going to continue we would either have to reduce our bakery range – or go nationally, and as a family we decided we didn't have the resources to do that. There were several people interested but we sold to Warburton's, a company that owned a number of shops in the north [of the UK]. The Mountstevens name stayed as part of the deal, but in July 2002, the new firm suddenly went bust.

# 227-231 KEITH POPLE LTD
(NOW THE LOUNGE)

**Pople's clothing shops were a once-familiar sight on Bristol's high streets with branches from Avonmouth to Fishponds, but the first shop to open was 227-229 North Street.** Keith Pople originally worked in an outfitters shop in Burnham-on-Sea. Hearing there was a business for sale in Bristol, he decided to pay a visit on a Saturday and see what the trade was really like. At the time, the shops in question were being run by Mrs Isaac, widow of George Isaac, who was unable to cope on her own and had decided to sell the business to Keith Pople. Apparently he paid £300 for the stock [1950s price].

Phyllis Neale went to work at the shop in 1962 when she was 42. Although

An aerial view of the longest row of shops along North Street. The original 1904 plan was predominantly housing

she retired in 1982, she remembers 'Mr Keith' and the shop well.

*I heard they wanted somebody at weekends. I started off doing Friday afternoon and all day Saturdays and it was cash in hand. It was a men's outfitters and they sold everything a man wanted. In one shop he had jeans and trousers and in the other shop he had knitwear, shirts and underwear.*

*Then it was decided that Clarke's shoes would go where the jeans and trousers were and so there was an opening put in the wall. Later on Mr Keith bought the shop next door (231) and had it made into a baby shop. The manageress of the shoe shop lived in the flat above. She was Mrs Roberts and her husband, Bill, was a Bristol City footballer. They lived there for years.*

Looking to expand his business, Keith Pople opened his next shop at the far end of North Street (20), opposite the Rex Cinema. According to Phyllis Neale 'it was another gents' outfitters but sold school uniforms, probably when comprehensive schools started – Withywood, Hartcliffe, Redcliffe, Merrywood, Ashton Park – practically every school in Bristol. Whatever school, Mr Keith would try and get it for customers. When the manager was on holiday I used to go there and look after the shop.'

Phyllis has some great stories about her experiences serving customers.

*The first man I ever served was an Irishman who was drunk. Anyway I stuck it and I enjoyed serving men or serving ladies, but not serving men and ladies together because one would like the item and the other wouldn't. The one that stood out in my mind was a man and woman came in and he wanted a shirt and tie to go with his waistcoat. The waistcoat had a peach colour in it and I was good at picking out colours so I showed him a shirt which was made of Crimplene and he said 'I like that.' The lady said 'You can't wear that to a wedding – it's Crimplene! Let's go down to Bedminster and get something else.' I thought to myself, 'No way, Missus am I going to stand here three quarters of an hour and let you go out without buying something!' Eventually he went out with the Crimplene shirt and tie and loved it.*

*There isn't much you can't tell me about shirts or trousers. I had an old man in one day and he wanted a pair of trousers so I said 'Do you know your inside leg [measurement]?' and he said 'No, but you can measure it because I'm helpless.' Another man came in and asked 'Have you got a pair of underpants that are supported because I'm well-blessed.' So I said 'Aren't you lucky you're well-blessed cos there aren't many men who can say that!' I always got on well with customers. I used to come down to their level.*

*How times have changed. I met a couple last year and the man was*

wearing a leather jacket that cost £600 and his jeans were £200! I used to sell jeans that were 19/11d [99p]. He had a Ben Sherman shirt that he said cost £60 and I used to sell them for 29/11d [£1.50].*

Phyllis recalls the manager's name was Don Melton. 'We used to have so much fun. He was a very shy person really. Every time I had a birthday he did a card for me. I could always lay the law down because he knew whatever I said I meant. There was Mrs Roberts and Mrs Lewis in the shoe shop, Don Melton and myself and Mrs Pinniger and then we took on Mrs Iris Webb who worked in Lions Store. We were always very busy and we did very well. Shoplifters were not unknown: 'They'd take braces, socks, ties.'

The shop did well as a result of the severe flooding in the area in 1968. 'When we had the floods in Duckmoor Road we were getting the shop ready for a sale. We simply didn't have enough stock because everyone in the floods only had the clothes they stood up in so they came in to buy more. We had a fantastic sale!'

Despite having a number of shops throughout Bristol, Keith Pople was a regular visitor at the North Street shop, as Phyllis Neale recalls:

*Everybody knew Mr Keith Pople. He used to come on a Saturday and go in the shop next door and buy plums, sprouts or whatever left over from the day before because it was cheaper. He was a very smart man, always had a nice suit on and a trilby, a slim face, a lovely man. He idolised his wife and he used to talk to me about her. He had two sons: the eldest one was a doctor*

*and went to America. The younger one, Donald although he was a barrister he eventually took over the business. I finished when I was 62 and I enjoyed every minute of it.*

In 1998, John Pople, Keith Pople's son, was awarded the Nobel Prize in Chemistry.

## 235 FRASER ANDREWS, WATCH AND CLOCK MAKERS AND JEWELLERS
(NOW MACK DADDY'S, HAIRDRESSERS)

☞ **Now a hairdresser's, this shop is unusual in being one of a row of eight properties set back from the road, which were originally built as houses.** Jill Sims's family ran a business here for over 60 years, starting when her grandfather, Francis Andrews, bought the house. He then converted part of it for his watch-making and repair business, along with an optician's at the back. He had already been running the business at number 71 in the 1920s and made the move along the road later that decade. Jill was born in 1949 and was brought up there, living over the shop with her mother Verona, father Raymond Herwig and her grandfather.

Jill has vivid memories of her grandfather and home life:

*At the back to the right of the shop there was a long passage and a room off that. Then there was the breakfast room, kitchen and another room behind and an outside toilet and a shed, and then there were stairs upstairs. There*

(Top) Jill Sims' grandfather, Francis Andrews, sitting on his high stool in the window. Probably taken c1930, the signboard reads 'Established 1900' and 'From 71 North Street', Francis' previous shop. Right is Joshua Williams' hosiery shop, and left is Stanley Blackwell, fruiterer (233); mistletoe and a Christmas tree appear to be hanging from the corbel

(Bottom) Jill Sims' parents Verona and Raymond Herwig and their wedding guests in the back garden of the family shop, 235 North Street. Front row, R to L: Francis Andrews (shop owner), Verona Herwig (daughter of Francis), Raymond Herwig (husband of Verona), Reg Andrews (son of Francis). Back row, R to L: Albert Christian Herwig (father of Raymond), Dorothy Herwig (mother of Raymond)

were another two flights up. I slept at the top at one time and could see the City ground from my bedroom window. Grandfather was well-known in the local neighbourhood and drove an Austin 'Ruby', a classic car of its time.

When Francis's wife fell ill their daughter Verona 'gave up work to nurse her, and when she died Mum carried on in the shop,' says Jill. Jill's mother Verona managed the retail side of the business, as Jill recalls:

There was a display case with gold jewellery in it. We sold clocks, jewellery, chains and there would be some sort of plastic necklaces – we used to call them 'poppets'. Mr Garraway, the rep, used to bring things in and Mum would decide what she wanted and make a list, then get me to check the adding up. This was in the 1950s and 60s.

Christmas had mixed memories for Jill. 'Mum was always busy at Christmas because people couldn't find what they wanted in town so they'd come to the local shop. The shop opposite Andrew's [number 250] has always been a butchers. Every Christmas Eve my Mum would supply Mr and Mrs Lye and the staff there with a tray of tea as they were so busy.' However, Jill's other memory of one Christmas in the 1950s is less pleasant:

There was a gas leak and a fire ignited. It was Christmas time and we'd been out visiting so we were up late. Suddenly there was a terrific bang and we saw these flames going up. The fireman said if we'd been in bed we might not have got out. The fire was so serious that I had to go and sleep at my friend's across the road at Ross's supermarket [number 236] on the corner of Exeter Road.

With Jill as a young girl helping out in the shop ('I used to go out into the shop and talk to customers'), there were three generations of the family at work. 'My grandfather did the watch repairs,' says Jill, 'then after he died [in 1966] my mum took on changing watch straps and batteries. When my father retired he did clock repairs, so he had one of the bedrooms upstairs as his workroom.' Apparently Jill's Dad 'used to make clocks out of saucepans and things like that.'

Family life was in the shop and the local community. 'When things were busy, Mum used to send me shopping, because she was always in the shop,' remembers Jill. Jill saw it as 'a good community, like it is now. But when the shops shut, North Street would be dead at night.' However Jill recalls that at one time the shop 'had burglaries and my dad used to put on a radio in the back to deter burglars. They'd got in the back and when the radio came on they dropped all the bags and boxes!' Others were out at night too, though probably not as late. Phyllis Neale recalls, as a youngster, that 'when we were kids at night the man would be sat one side of the shop repairing watches and on the other side was an elderly lady knitting socks. She had a little machine and she'd wind the wool around, and we used to sit and watch her.'

In the 1970s, says Jill, 'business went downhill when Wills' closed, but Mum kept going. She had someone to collect the repairs, but she would put watch straps on. Finally, though, we closed because Mum was in care.'

# 245 THE DINKIE
(NOW PERSONIC COMPUTERS)

 **First appearing in the 1921 street directory as William Alfred Sansom, artificial teeth maker, by 1930 Mr Sansom was described as 'Dentist', obviously acquiring the necessary qualifications in the intervening years.** By 1939, the shop had changed to a tobacconists run by George Stanley Shaxton, recalled by Mervyn Southway: 'There was one man on his own and he was a bit deaf so all the boys used to call him 'Deafie'. Used to sell sweets, tobacco, and carbonated water from a machine for a halfpenny.'

The shop was taken over in 1956 by George White who kept the name 'The Dinkie', painted in red letters on the yellow shop front, as it was so well-known in the area. George's son John takes up the story:

*My father involved me from the start. The opening hours were from seven in the morning until ten at night, seven days a week! In those days you had a load of people coming out of Wills' and we also had good trade from the Plaza Cinema. On Friday afternoons we used to have queues outside the shop waiting to get in – people from Wills'. There were three or four of us serving and we did really good business. Then after a few years my father said 'This is worse than the milk round!' so he started cutting down the hours when the shop was open.*

*After I'd done a day's work, I used to help out in the evenings and at weekends. When I was 22, I had to do my National Service and after training*

*I was posted to Headley Park so I was able to still help out in the shop quite a lot. My father and mother did a very good job at building up the business which had a very good selection of loose sweets and chocolates. They also sold tobacco and cigarettes and Walls' ice cream which was a big novelty when rationing stopped. After three years my father started to cut back the [opening] hours and eventually got it to six in the evenings and then cut out Sunday afternoons.*

*My father gave me the choice of working for him otherwise he was going to sell up. I decided that I would do it, but I knew there was no way that the shop was going to keep me as well. However, I was able to get some money working in the afternoons for Mr Tucker who had a fish and chip shop (283) and also did wholesale papers. I worked for him every afternoon for about three*

John White of The Dinkie (245) discussing cigarette sales with his father

John White behind the counter of The Dinkie (245), a vast array of sweets on display

hours as well as Sunday mornings from around 2am to 10am doing the country run.

My father was very good and gave me a free hand. He arranged a larger overdraft and first of all we decided to start selling pipes, lighters and leather goods. My father's thing was he never did what everyone else did – he would try something different. Eventually I got married and it was at this time that we started selling Hallmark cards. This was round about 1964. It was a complete success right from the start. Just before this we had the passage wall knocked down to make more space and then within a year of starting selling cards we had the back wall knocked down with help from a couple of customers. We began work on a Saturday night at six,

closed all day Sunday and were open for business as usual on the Monday morning.

My wife, Ann, used to choose which umbrellas to sell and we sold loads, also walking sticks. We had a few pipes which cost £200! They would be briars and might last for 20 to 30 years. Our main supplier of fancy goods, leather goods and pipes were Hall and Fitzgerald's of Hotwells Road. We also went on to sell a large range of Lindt chocolates and we were known to be a specialist tobacconist – one of only three in Bristol. Our theory was we sold good quality stuff at reasonable prices. We eventually got rid of the ice cream as the electric for the freezers was costing us more than we were actually making.

During this time I was only working for

him for the first few years but then he took me on as a partner. When I finally took over, my father would always come in every day. After he died it became 'J & AT White' but we always kept the name of The Dinkie. The AT was my wife, Ann Thelma.

John retired in 2003 and although the business kept going for a further six years, The Dinkie finally ceased trading in 2009.

# 257 GINO'S CAFÉ
(NOW PIMM'S PIZZA)

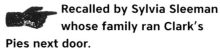 **Recalled by Sylvia Sleeman whose family ran Clark's Pies next door.**

It was named after the man who ran it. He was in his 20s and I think he had a brother called Tino. Gino had not long been married and he brought his family over to the café. His wife couldn't speak a word of English so I befriended her. I can't remember her name but she used to cook lovely sponges. One day one of our girls went in and she gave her a glass of wine and I can still see Lesley staggering about!

It was just an egg and chips sort of café, nothing spectacular, but very busy because of all the Wills' girls. I used to go in and help at lunchtimes and we were very busy. Being Italian they did coffees like espresso. For the local traders who wanted a hot meal and didn't want to sit in the café, they'd put a lid over the food and would deliver it to their shop. I remember a tiny sink where we used to wash the dishes.

Gino and his family were very nice people. They were only there for a couple of years. I think he bought another place in Bristol but don't know where.

# 259 CLARK'S PIES

The pie production team. Pasties are made upstairs

👉 **A real Bristol institution, Clark's Pies was established in North Street in 1932 by Harold Clark.** Sylvia Sleeman (nee Clark) recalls the early days.

*My grandmother, Mary, started a pie business in Cardiff over a hundred years ago. She was very poor, her husband was a drunkard and she had seven children so she had to do something to get them fed. She was a very good cook who started making pies for the neighbours and it grew from there. As the children grew up they helped out and then took over. My father, Harold Percy Clark, first opened a pie shop in Hanham with my mother Nellie, but decided to move to North Street when I was about three months old in 1932. I've no idea why they chose North Street. It may have been because the property was cheaper, or it could have been because of the nearby Wills factory and all the hungry workers there.*

The business appears in the 1939 Bristol Street directory as Clark, Mrs Nellie Louisa, pie mkr.

Sylvia remembers the shop as a child:

*When I grew up, I used to serve in the shop and we were very, very busy. You'd have the queues right down the road. When the war came Dad couldn't join up because of his health so he joined the ARP as a fire warden, so Mum basically* helped him out and took over running the business.

*As meat was strictly rationed the firm switched to making 'Auntie Nellie's veggie pies' using vegetables from an allotment garden at Avonmouth. Coal was also in short supply, so at Christmas local people would bring their turkeys to be cooked in the shop oven and sometimes Sunday roasts as well.*

*Downstairs in what is now the bake-house was our living area with a little baking room behind it. As the business expanded we did away with our kitchen to make the bake-house bigger. Upstairs overlooking the street was our dining room where the pasties were made. We had masses of room upstairs and lived 'over the shop'.*

*We just did a steak and kidney pie and that was 3d and a savoury drier pasty which was 2d. That was all we ever sold. We didn't deliver, we just sold from the shop. Years ago there was no hatch: it was a big open counter and we had a big window in the front where we* used to put flowers.

Percy and Nellie's eldest son, John eventually took over the firm and when he retired in 1989, his brother Ken became manager. He in turn handed over to his younger brother, Roger. Today the family business is run by Roger's daughter, Dawn, and her partner Keith Prested who took over from Roger in 2007, becoming the fourth generation in charge. Keith describes the current operation:

*A traditional Clark's pie is essentially beef, potato, kidney, onion and seasoning in a short crust pastry. A pie costs £1.50. We do a steak and ale pie – diced skirt steak with mushrooms and onions and we use the Tobacco Factory's beer. We also make pasties which are beef and potato in short crust and flaky pastry. Sausage rolls and cheese, potato and onion pasties too. We probably make just over 1,000 items a day. We deliver all over Bristol, to fish and chip shops, pubs, butchers. We go north as far as Chipping Sodbury and*

**63**

The staff at Clark's Pies c1955, taken in the alleyway at the rear of the shop. L to R: Ken Clark; Mrs Clark (Nellie Louisa); Kay Bond (staff member); Sylvia Clark; John Clark, Violet ? (Staff member); Roger Clark; Harry Percy (staff member, always known as Percy)

*Yate; we deliver in Saltford, Portishead and Clevedon and during the summer season we'll go down to the caravan sites at Brean.*

*We have about 30 people working for us, some part time. Generally they work about three and a half hours a day; drivers work six hours a day. Some start work at 5.45am, the main bulk at 7.00 and the next shift at 7.30.*

Due to constraints of the building, the business still operates much as it has done for many years, albeit with modern cooking equipment. Behind the shop is the boiler room where the various fillings are assembled and the bake ovens; pasty production takes place on the first floor with the offices above.

# 269 ASHTON FRUIT SHOP

👉 **This parade of shops was built in the first decade of the 20th century, number 269 at one time being described a 'fried fish dealer' and then a 'piano importer'.** The Young family took the shop over as existing greengrocers in the late 1930s and their son Peter carried on the family business until the end of the twentieth century. Bob Wherlock remembers 'Mrs Young used to be on her hands and knees on a Saturday night scrubbing the floor,' and Phil Elliot recalls 'Mr Young always wore a brown overall and Mrs Young always wore a flowered overall. They seemed to speak very countrified. They would serve you – it was all behind the counter.' Clive Green remembers how 'Mrs Young was such a small woman but she'd pick up hundredweight [50 kilograms] bags of potatoes and haul them around the shop.'

After a period when the greengrocer's was run as Stokes, Mark Rudge and his brother Mike moved in to run the Ashton Fruit Shop. Mark says that he has been doing this kind of work 'pretty much since I left school.' After he and his brother had learnt the greengrocer's trade as employees here and in nearby East Street, they took over the shop in 2002. Their other brother Dave later joined the staff and completed the family business.

The brothers know their trade and customers and they pride themselves on the freshness of their produce, 'rarely having stock left over' at the end of the

day. 'I know you can get most things all the year round now,' says Mark, 'but people will still tend to buy seasonal produce. What people want certainly has changed. Broccoli is now more popular than cauliflower, whereas years ago it always used to be the other way round.' Some of their lines are both seasonal and local: 'Nearby farmers might come to us, or gardeners, with a crop of marrows or runner beans.'

Mark sells traditional lines, but he's had to move with the times too. What might have sounded exotic in Bedminster when the shop started now seems commonplace. 'Fresh figs sell pretty well at this time of the year, and butternut squash is becoming more and more popular.' If people come in and ask for unusual things – chicory perhaps, or banana leaves – they will always do their best. 'We ask them to give us a bit of notice and we can probably get it, just for them.' However, the Rudges are practical traders. For example, when people started asking them to stock organic food, they gave it a go. 'It started off alright.' said Mark, 'and we were selling quite a lot of it.' But then difficulties about labelling and other costs, made them decide this wasn't going to be successful.

Saturday is their busiest day and there is also a bit of a rush after the local primary school finishes in the afternoon, with parents in search of a healthy snack. Mark says they don't need to advertise or have a shop make-over. In fact, he says, 'not much has changed about the shop' since they began, apart from 'the trends of people buying different stuff.' Trade was quite vibrant when he started, and 'it's been pretty

The audience listen politely to story-telling amongst the vegetables by Angie Belcher. In 2009 Show of Strength Theatre Company's Trading Local 'Refreshed the parts of town centres other cultural activities fail to go anywhere near' with a mile of street performance. Business went on as normal around the actors

Mark Rudge, Ashton Fruit Shop (269)

much a steady rate of trade since we took over, perhaps busier than it used to be.' Mark puts it down to several reasons. 'People like to shop local' he says. Mark doesn't see the supermarket over the road as a big threat to trade. 'It brings car-driving customers to the area. If a customer has a big box, we generally carry it to their car for them and we carry a lot of shopping over to the Aldi car park!'

Apart from providing good service and fresh produce, what is Mark's explanation for their success? 'Greengrocers don't go out of fashion,' says Mark. 'Everyone's got to eat – you can try and make your clothes last longer, make your shoes last, you don't have to have your hair cut so often , but everyone's got to eat.'

# 275 ASHTON CINEMA

(NOW OCEAN, ESTATE AGENTS AND RESIDENTIAL)

 **Although much changed, this is one of the last two remaining cinema buildings in Bedminster, and was built in 1914 as the Ashton Cinema.** It was the first of the five cinemas in the area, which were later to include the Rex (**see 19-25**) at the opposite end of North Street.

In the 1930s the cinema was owned by a Mr Atkinson who also ran the Bedminster Town Hall and Redcliffe cinemas. Mrs E Smith was an usherette at the time:

*It was quite a nice, clean, cheerful*

*place. They opened evenings from six o'clock until ten o'clock and also a Saturday matinee. Attendance was pretty good, especially Saturday nights when one could be sure of a full house. Seats were mostly booked, and always young couples, who came every week, so one got to know them well. There were changes of pictures each week, besides the Pathe News. These pictures and newsreels were passed on to the Town Hall Cinema and the Redcliffe, and a young man who worked with the projectionist would get on his bike to deliver them. The piano was played at each of the cinemas and the pianist followed the pictures around. So at Ashton, we saw three pianists a week. The pictures were black and white with words coming up on the screen. Old Westerns with Tom Mix, or pictures that made one weep, or comics accompanied by piano music.*

Many people remember the children's films during Saturday's 'tuppenny rush', so called because 'they opened the door and in everyone rushed.' John Hardingham, recalling the 1930s, worked hard for his Saturday ticket,

**65**

saying that 'I used to run errands for people – sometimes to give a message to someone and they would give me tuppence.' Edna Beake also 'ran errands and minded babies,' to earn her tuppence. She got her money's worth as she and her two friends 'pushed into a double seat.' Phyllis Neale remembers 'how it was all silent films. You had Mrs Pope playing the piano and Miss Shellard was the usherette.' Phil Elliot also remembers the busy staff: 'The manager was a man called Ted Leigh and he had one usherette, Nell Knott, and his son. Ted used to show the film, then in the interval he'd come and help with the ice creams and he'd take the money.' Even more helpful was Mrs Bolt, as Diana Brown recalls: 'Dad and I used to go on a Monday night and we'd get in for free because we knew Mrs Bolt who sold the tickets.'

People remember how the films might be changed up to three times a week: 'so you'd go to the Town Hall [cinema] one day and up there the next.' Muriel and Ken Eley can recall seeing Flash Gordon, Tarzan and Our Gang, and Mervyn Southway remembers 'the cowboy films, cartoons, and Charlie Chaplin.' Edna Beake also remembers the silent films: 'We really enjoyed the serial, it was such a treat. During the interval the lights go up and we all sit back and discuss what we had seen, and share my halfpenny worth of monkey nuts.' Jack House's 'real thrill of going to the Ashton Cinema' came in 1953 when, as he remembers:

*I represented the Boys' Brigade at the Coronation. I was stationed outside Buckingham Palace when the official film was made. As the Queen's carriage*

c1959, the Plaza is closed for good, still advertising its final film, Blue Murder at St Trinians. In December 1958 a week's films had included The Fuzzy Pink Nightgown (starring Jane Russell), Beach Head (Tony Curtis) and Revolt at Fort Laramie. EF Bull's sweet shop (273) is just visible to the left

*swept around the Albert Memorial there's a shot of me, and I actually saw it for the first time in the Ashton Cinema!*

Ashton Cinema, or the Plaza as it became around 1954, was neither as big nor as prestigious as its more recently-built rivals. Jack House remembers the cinema in this period:

*I suppose it seated about 150 people downstairs. Then there was the balcony and the projection box in the middle and about a dozen seats either side. One of the problems was the noise emanating from the projector. If you sat in the balcony you couldn't hear anything projected onto the screen.*

'I don't think they got up to date films, it was the end of the run. At the Rex you had a commissionaire outside but you didn't have that at the Ashton',

recall Sheila and Glyn Williams and Frank Phillips remembers it as 'a small cinema which showed old films and horror films. It was a bit of a flea pit.' Pat Stiles remembers 'going there with my Mum and Dad. They used to squirt perfume around, well I think that's what it was. It was probably disinfectant.'

The behaviour of the children was sometimes a little noisy, as Phyllis Neale remembers: 'If it was cowboys and Indians and the Indians were coming up behind the cowboys we used to shout "they're behind you!"' Bernard and Alma Chalmers remember more unruly companions: 'They were a rough lot there, they used to throw everything at everybody – orange rind, papers.' Finally, after fifty years or more, Rex Whitrow and Lew Pedlar are able to confess what

The upper floor of the Plaza cinema, awaiting refurbishment after the closure of the Paragon

really went on:

*The cinema provided us tearaways with some innocent fun. There was a lane that ran to the rear of the building. We used to throw stones at the corrugated iron cladding that projected out from the rear wall. It made a hell of a racket for the poor patrons and it soon alerted the manager whose red face and blistering verbals caused us to scamper away at great speed! I recall scoring a direct hit with a rocket launched out of a milk bottle one bonfire night.*

The peak year for cinema-going was 1949, audiences declining throughout the 1950s. The Plaza closed late that decade and by the mid-1960s the ground floor had opened as Quality Fare Supermarket. June Hodge was employed there in 1971:

*It was the first sort of mini-supermarket. It was a mess: everything was stacked up. I stacked shelves in the evenings because there wasn't late-closing in those days. It was a private*

owner. All the girls who worked there were local.*

Above the shop, reached by a stairway from North Street, was the Paragon Snooker Club, a decidedly shady place, as one local resident remembers:

*One night I went down there, I must have been 16, going on 17. They used to have a bit of an illegal card school in a little back room and I got stitched. There was me and me mate, we knew it was being done but we had to take it on the chin. That was on a Friday night we used to go there. When you actually lose the best part of a week's wages, it cures you of gambling. We used to go to play snooker there but there was a "character" there. I can't mention names. I wouldn't say he was a thug but he certainly had his entourage. We used to go for a game of snooker but then people would come up and put £5 on the table for a bit of a bet, trying to set you up in a game.*

Another young man at the time also remembers it 'had quite a notorious name. I was playing snooker there once and someone told me they needed cash and to go into this [back] room. When I went in there I'd never seen so much money on the table. I was told in no uncertain terms to "go somewhere" – in other words, I shouldn't have poked my nose in there.'

At some point the Paragon closed, while downstairs the Quality Fare Supermarket was replaced by Imperial Carpets and when they moved to nearby West Street, the whole building was subject of major refurbishment. Once completed in 2008, Bristol estate agents Ocean took over the ground floor, the upper part of the former cinema having being converted to flats, fittingly named The Plaza Apartments.

The Paragon Snooker & Billiards sign still hangs above the carpet store, closed before its renovation

# RALEIGH ROAD TO ST FRANCIS ROAD 277-283

A tram stops opposite the Tobacco Factory, nearing the terminus in Ashton Road. The service ran to and from Bristol Bridge, and early workers could catch the first tram at 5.25am, with the last tram arriving back at 11.15pm. The Ashton Floral Depot sign was above Gertrude Brayley's fruit shop on the corner of Raleigh Road and North Street. c1935-1939

**T**he name Raleigh Road provides a link with the tobacco industry which once flourished in this part of Bristol as presumably it was named after Sir Walter Raleigh, reputedly the first person to bring tobacco back to this country. The short terrace of four shops is characterised by the tall brick facades of the buildings which mirror the former Franklin Davey factory on the other side of North Street.

On the corner is one of several restaurants in this part of North Street, Souk Kitchen (277), established in 2010 and a link to when the building housed 'refreshment rooms' run by William England in the 1920s. The restaurant specialises in North African and Mediterranean food. The next door premises, now Eddy's Domestic Appliances (**see 279**), for many years housed a dairy run by John Cox from the 1920s to 1950s, then becoming a

# 279 EDDY'S DOMESTIC APPLIANCES

 **When Dave Bjelica and his brother Ron were youngsters they couldn't keep away from their Dad's workshop, helping Eddy repair domestic appliances for the family shop.** Starting in the 1970s, the Bjelicas, father and sons, built up a loyal following in their east Bristol shop. With business going well, the family expanded by opening a shop in Ashton in 1991.

'It wasn't any easy start', says Dave. North Street was still in the downturn from the closure of the Wills tobacco factories. However, trade gradually improved, and when the Aldi supermarket opened over the road, Dave says that business virtually doubled. His philosophy is that more people in the area can only be better for trade. On a Sunday, Dave might be found having a coffee in the cafe opposite. Sometimes he spots shoppers peering through his shop window but he feels there is no need to open the shop. Mondays are his busiest day of the week.

Dave has a theory about the cause of this steady improvement in trade over the last 20 years. 'It's partly how the area has changed,' he explains, 'there is simply more money around.' He has also been a good businessman, responding to the shift from people wanting repairs and 'something cheap.' Nowadays 95% of his sales are new equipment. Above all, Dave and his team of around fourteen staff pride themselves on offering old-fashioned service. Several staff have worked for the firm for over 20 years and it is still a family business with family values. If customers are stuck he says 'we will do our darnedest to help someone.

A broken washing machine for the older person can be the end of the world and we want them to rest assured.' It's not unknown for Dave to turn a blind eye to the call-out fee for 'an old lady who rings up in tears and says her cooker is broken – only to find the switch is off.' In Dave's words, he and his staff 'put ourselves out for local people. We want to give the personal touch.'

Has this approach helped him weather the recession, or is it just sentimental? Dave is very confident that selling on service and not just price is his winning ticket. He can tell when someone comes in to look but intends to seek a better price on the internet. It doesn't worry him. The majority of people who do this, he says, 'end up buying from me instead!' Eddy's is the firm where you can have your washing machine delivered the same day, taken up awkward stairs and installed. There's no need for him to advertise. Having an excellent reputation is the company's reward and their best selling-point.

Dave Bjelica, proprietor of Eddy's Domestics, 2013

Wedding cake ideas at Occasion Cakes (281), 2013

branch of Wrington Vale Dairies.

Occasion Cakes (281) opened in August 1996 and is run by Nicky Lanfear and a small team. Nicky originally started out on her own, when necessary helped out by friends and members of her family. The business creates about 12 to 15 cakes a day, six days a week, customers coming from all over Bristol and as far away as Wales. 'We sell more cakes for children than adults – not surprising really' says Nicky. 'People love cakes. It's an excuse to celebrate!'

For some 40 years number 281 was occupied by Henry Dando, a popular men's hairdresser. The last shop in this terrace is the Willow Garden which sells takeaway Chinese and other foods. The shop has a long history of providing 'fast food'. William Iles operated a fried fish business here in the 1920s and Mrs Laura Green plied the same trade in the 1930s. After a spell as a newsagents run by Edgar Tucker in the 1940s and 50s, by 1962 the shop was once again selling fish and chips, still owned by Mr Tucker until 1973 when the owners of the Willow Garden took over the business.

# ST FRANCIS ROAD TO ASHTON ROAD 291-295

CHAPTER 14

**T**he large building on the corner of St Francis Road – formerly the Regent Tyre and Rubber Company, tyre re-moulders, and later on a car repair garage – is The Brewery Theatre, a thriving performance venue, café and bar, run as an off-shoot of The Tobacco Factory. The far end of the building houses Mark's Bread (**see 291**).

The entrance alongside Mark's Bread leads in to a large yard, now called Brewery Court, surrounded by a collection of late nineteenth century industrial buildings, originally constructed as the Ashton Gate Brewery. Brewing was started on this site by Thomas Baynton and his brothers in the first decades of the nineteenth century, a map of the area in 1840 confirming this. The Ashton Gate Brewery which produced the well-known 'Sunrise' ('Outshines Them All!') was eventually taken over by Georges & Co. in 1931 and wound up two years later when all its assets and pubs were handed over to Georges, at which point brewing ceased.

MANUFACTURERS OF CORPORATION
**DECK CHAIRS**
WIND BREAKS
BATHING TENTS
SIDE FOLDING
ARM CHAIRS

"YBRO" WHITEWOOD BEDROOM & KITCHEN FURNITURE
"STORMASTER" TRANSPORT TARPAULINS
INDUSTRIAL TEXTILE FABRICATORS — MARQUEE HIRE CONTRACTORS
**YEO** BROS. **PAULL** LTD
NORTH STREET - ASHTON GATE - BRISTOL 3
Phone: BRISTOL 664294/8

Following closure, the brewery buildings were put to various uses over the years, a noted occupant being Yeo Bros Paull who supplied marquees and canvas tarpaulins. Dave Russell remembers going there on his delivery rounds: 'We used to deliver the materials to make marquees. I remember going in one day and this young lad was putting the eyes [metal rivets along the canvas edges of marquees] in and he took the top of his thumb off!' The firm, which began life as W Yeo and Sons, rope makers, in Teignmouth, Devon, expanded its business to Bristol in 1901. It was later bought by William Henry Paull who kept the name Yeo and established the company headquarters at Martock, Somerset, the North Street premises continuing as part of the business.

Another one-time occupant of these buildings was HW Carter & Co., the company which produced Ribena. This popular drink made from blackcurrants was invented in Bristol at the National Fruit and Cider Institute based in Long Ashton, and was originally intended as a

The 12th Battalion Gloucestershire Regiment marching towards Ashton Gate, in front of St Francis's Church. The Franklyn Davey tobacco factory top left. c1914

vitamin C supplement, the concentrated syrup being mixed with water to make a healthy drink. Production of Ribena continued in Bristol for several years until production was relocated to the Forest of Dean.

The revival of the brewing industry on the site began in 2004 when The Bristol Beer Factory started production. Business is booming, as the managing director, Simon Bartlett explains: 'We make five main cask beers and a further ten bottled varieties, our best sellers being 'Southville Hop', 'Milk Stout' and 'Seven'. Brewing takes place in the tall red brick building, constructed in 1903 as the New Fermenting Block, and the brewery supplies beers to a number of outlets, among which are the adjacent Brewery Theatre, the Tobacco Factory, the Grain Barge moored along Anchor Road, and the Barley Mow in St Philips.

It is clear from plans of the original brewery that all the buildings beyond what is now Brewery Court were all part of the brewing complex. The first building nowadays houses Workout Gym, beyond which a stone-pillared entrance leads to another former industrial work yard and a delightful collection of single storey Victorian buildings, now converted to business units. Of special note along this final stretch of North Street is the unusual metal-edged curbing, designed to protect the pavement from the wear and tear of the metal-rimmed wheels of the dray carts with their heavy loads.

# 291 MARK'S BREAD

**Mark Newman's artisan bakery has queues out of the door every Saturday and has brought a fresh aroma to this end of North Street.** Local car drivers recall paying for their MOT here in what was once the reception office of Nationwide Autocentre, but it is now what must be one of the smallest bakeries in Bristol.

Mark set up his business at a turning point in both his life – and that of North Street too. Mark and his partner Maria have lived in the area for 30 years. 'I've always liked North Street', says Mark, 'but it has changed. Twenty years ago you couldn't buy an aubergine and there was only one restaurant in south Bristol.' For his fiftieth birthday, Maria bought Mark a two day bread-making course and on the second day, while taking sourdough bread out of the wood-fired oven, Mark decided that what he really wanted to do was to set up a local bakery. 'I knew the time was right; there was a demand for the kind of bread you can buy in Germany or France, but nowhere here.' He gave up his job and rented a kitchen for six months, baking 'about 50 loaves a week, going round to neighbours and friends on the bike with sacks of bread on the handlebars.' At this stage, 'I was thinking of [renting] an industrial unit. I wasn't looking for a shop on the high street, I wanted to bake bread, but not run a shop, perhaps doing markets.'

In 2009 Mark was offered the tiny unused space alongside the newly-opened Brewery Theatre, so he took this on, still intending it to be just a bakery. 'The big door was just to get the oven in, not as a shop.' By Christmas that year and with a couple of steady trade orders, Mark had started retailing:

*I just put up a piece of paper on the door saying 'Bread for Sale.' I wanted to do it like that – I didn't want to have a big splash and then find the product wasn't consistent. Initially it was just me. When I was out on my bike delivering, I just had a note on the door saying 'Back in 5 Minutes'.*

Working single-handed was difficult in those first weeks.

*I put up a sign saying you can order bread for Christmas Eve and it was probably my worst day. I got up at 3am, with people coming at 10am. I was trying to get the baguettes out of the oven and customers get quite stressed at Christmas. I remember one guy being irate because I ruined his Christmas dinner because he didn't have the rye bread to go with his salmon!*

It wasn't long before offers of help came in and Mark's business flourished. He is not at all pretentious about what he is doing and has developed a successful business model. He doesn't advertise:

*They'll come back if they like it, not if you have a glossy advert, my marketing is in the community. For example, I had school kids in from the primary school over the road, 6 year olds. It's nice for them to be aware of how food should be, and it is tactile. And their mums might come in and buy some bread!*

Another aspect of Mark's approach came from his observations of North Street before he set up his bakery:

*Bob Wherlock [now Rare Meat] was a good business model. You'd be in the queue, there would be banter with Bob and his staff, you'd bump into people, a social time, that's what shopping should be. People come in and they smell the bread and it reminds them of their childhood – bread and community.*

There is also a kind of intentional 'theatre' to the business:

*What you get from the layout in the shop is a response from the customers while you are baking because you are there. That's why we don't do nights. I wanted to have hot bread coming out of the oven in the morning for customers to see.*

Mark has the quiet enthusiasm of someone who has wanted to do this for many years:

*There is something very comforting and soothing about making bread. It's a bit magical turning flour and water into something quite complicated and completely different – a living process. Once you mix the yeast and the flour it has begun and you follow it through to*

the end. *It fitted what I wanted to do –
something that was fulfilling for me and
that I was enthusiastic about.*

Although people ask 'Are you getting
too big? Have you thought about
expanding?' this is not how Mark sees
his work: 'I think that it has to be small
or you lose touch with the process.'
The sturdy 'Breadmobile' delivery bike
with its basket of loaves is a symbol of
what Mark's Bread is about. So, with
the 'theatre' of bread-making alongside
the Brewery Theatre, and the smell of
yeast from the brewery behind mingling
with that of Southville Sourdough, Mark
sums up the business as 'something in
the high street – being part of that, the
butcher, the theatre, something that
is local, giving people a choice about
what they can eat. There is a good bit
of banter going on – it does seem to
give people a smile on their face.'

Mark Newman takes a break from serving
customers with free slices cut from South
Bristol's longest loaf. Baked in May 2014 for
the South Bristol Arts Trail, the bakery also
opened its oven doors to local people for use
as a 'community oven'

# CHAPTER 15

# ASHTON TOLL HOUSE TO ASHTON GATE TERRACE 312-294

**T**he distinctive Toll House building marks the start of the second side of North Street. Beyond the Toll House is a short terrace of houses, once known as St Alban's Cottages, intersected by Back Lane and Ashton Gate Terrace. This might seem on the fringe of retailing in North Street, but at one time there were six shops here and two are still in use: Bristol Bound, bookbinders and El Rincon, a Spanish bar.

On the corner of Back Lane, number 302 was a barbers shop called Hoddinott's for at least 60 years before being converted to a house. Legend has it that Stan Laurel, the British half of the famous 'Laurel and Hardy' comedy act, had his hair cut here while he and Oliver Hardy were appearing at the Bristol Hippodrome on one of their UK tours in the 1930s. Unlikely though this may seem, there was a noted guesthouse, frequented by visiting stage artists, in nearby Coronation Road, so it is possible that 'Laurel and Hardy' were staying there when Stan popped round the corner for a quick trim!

Crossing Back Lane (formerly Britannia Place), the next rank of shops at one time included bakers, confectioners, newsagents and grocers.

Phil Elliot was a paper boy for Graham's newsagents (298): 'We used to help each other out if one was short. There wasn't any rivalry because we all had our own territories. You wouldn't deliver on someone else's patch.' The shop is now El Rincon, 'a little corner of Spain in the heart of BS3', as owner Dave Wilson describes it.

By the 1940s, the shops here included a chemists, selling non-prescription medicines, which according to Lew Pedlar was run by Marion Keest. Malcolm Pearce remembers his grandparents running the wool shop (294) around this time.

# CHAPTER 16

# ASHTON GATE TERRACE TO GREENWAY BUSH LANE 292-278

**T**he terrace of ten houses from Ashton Gate Terrace to the primary school, is evidence of the housing boom which took place in this part of Bristol in the closing years of the nineteenth century, planning permission being granted for the development here in 1889.

A baker's shop (292) run by Josef Zohrer in the 1960s and 1970s, stood on the corner of Ashton Gate Terrace.

The shop was very popular and people still remember its proprietor, described as 'a gentle Polish émigré', and 'a big chap, very friendly'. By all accounts, Zohrer was an excellent baker. Muriel Eley recalls the shop with its 'scrubbed shelves, filled with loaves.' Dave Russell, who used to deliver sacks of flour, Mary Cookson and her sister Jane, as well as Jill Sims all remember 'pies that would melt in your mouth', the 'freshly-made

sausage rolls and cakes' and 'the most delicious buns, pastries and pies. Their custard tarts were 'to die for!'

Jack House, former vicar of St Francis's Church, has a particular reason to remember Zohrer's:

*On Maundy Thursday we always had a sleepover in the church hall with the youngsters. This would be on the Thursday night until Good Friday [when we would] go across to Zohrer's and get a basket of hot cross buns. We had a wonderful time!*

By the time Hank [Julian] Hancock was working at the bakers in the early 1980s, it 'was run by Bev and his wife Dot. I used to help out when they were short of staff.' Hank remembers how:

*When I went in the morning, I would get the bread out of the ovens to cool. This would be about 6am and the bakers would have finished by then. I would slice the bread and make up the orders. My main job was doing deliveries. He had a 1954 Morris ambulance, sprayed green – the same colour as the outside of the shop. It had air suspension which wouldn't damage the bread if I had to brake quickly! One of my jobs would be to fill the doughnuts with jam. We had a square box with a lid on which was a T-shaped tube. I would put a doughnut on the end, push the handle down and jam would come up into the doughnut. "Only one squirt, mind", Bev would say to me.*

1889 Building plan for 292 North Street, on the corner of Ashton Gate Terrace. Originally proposed as an end-of-terrace house, the application was changed to a corner shop, which later became Zohrer's bakers shop. One hundred years later, the shop has been converted to residential use

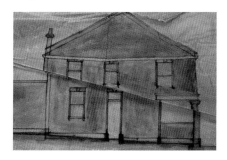

CHAPTER 17

# GREENWAY BUSH LANE TO RALEIGH ROAD

Bristol Mayor George Ferguson joins the beginning of the procession for the 2014 Bristol Festival of Puppetry, outside the Tobacco Factory

**D**uring the last fifteen years, this section of North Street has undergone the most significant developments which have played a major part in the overall regeneration of the street. From the early twentieth century until the 1990s, the land between Greenway Bush Lane and Raleigh Road was occupied by a vast factory complex, part of the Imperial Tobacco Company empire. The distinctive red brick building with the entwined initials, 'FD' carved in terracotta above the main entrance on Raleigh Road, was constructed in 1912 for Messrs Franklyn Davey and later subsumed by WD & HO Wills whose vast Number Three factory fronted Raleigh Road to the junction with Upton Road. A further building on North Street, constructed in the 1960s, housed the company's research laboratories. Alma Chalmers had an aunt who worked there: 'They were looking into new sorts

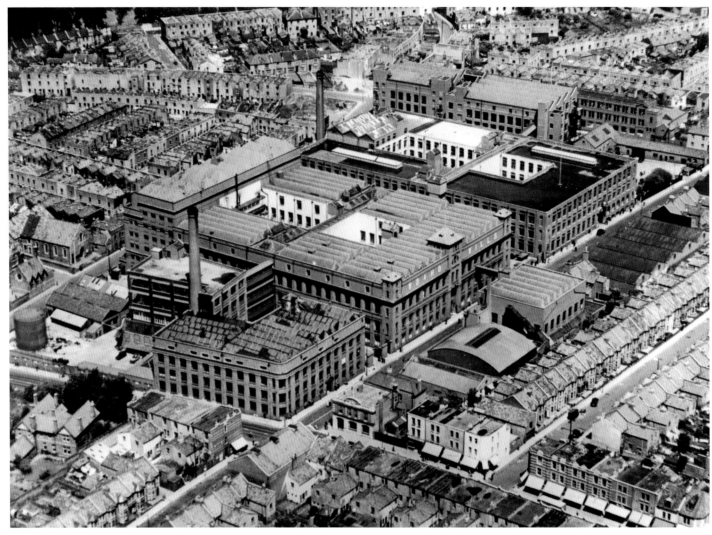

The vast cigarette production factories dominate this undated picture of the west end of North Street. Shop awnings were de rigeur

of cigarettes and passers-by would be invited in to test new blends of tobacco and rewarded for their effort with free cigarettes.'

Following the departure of the entire Imperial Tobacco operation from Bedminster in the 1970s, the premises lay empty for nearly twenty years until the main factory and laboratory building were demolished, paving the way for redevelopment of the site. A branch

of the budget-brand supermarket, Aldi, opened in 2000, attracting new shoppers to the area. Hearing that the Franklyn Davey building was also threatened with demolition, Bristol architect and entrepreneur George Ferguson stepped in and purchased it: 'It seemed criminal to knock these buildings down, which is what they were going to do, as they've got such fantastic quality – so that's what drove

me to buy it.'

First to open in the aptly-named Tobacco Factory was the Theatre: 'I wanted a place where everything from traditional Shakespeare to cutting edge new writing would be performed', says George Ferguson. 'It's just a rough, industrial space painted black and it's become a theatre.' Since its opening, the Tobacco Factory Theatre has gained national recognition for both the quality and innovative nature of the work performed there.

Part of the ground floor of the building was occupied for over ten years by Teoh's, a pan-Asian diner where the menu rarely changed, Tiger beer was always available and vegetarians could delight in the meals adapted for them, meat or fish simply replaced by tofu. The space is now home to the Thali Café. The remainder of the ground floor forms the Tobacco Factory Café/ Bar which opened five years after the Theatre. Like the Theatre, the Café/Bar is designed around the features of the building, giving it a distinctively industrial feel. 'I wanted the bar to be a buzzing place where everyone feels welcome', says George Ferguson. Anna Gilman has been the bar manager for five and a half years:

*The Bar's a fixture on North Street. It's changed so much since I started working here, both the type and amount of people. We get a lot of young families now and we're lucky with space as*

Xanthe Ivory in 2013, selling flowers from the Tobacco Factory entrance lobby, before moving to 228 North Street

*people can meet each other without worrying about buggies. If you've got decent coffee it encourages people to meet. We don't feel in competition with the other cafés and bars. We have a really good relationship with each other. If we run out of coffee beans we run*

*up to the next place and ask them to help. The Bristol Beer Factory supplies our ales. We've always had a simple menu and have tried to keep it basic but tasty, and people seem to like it. We get busy before the theatre shows and lunchtimes. On match days we allow both sides in, but tend to get family groups, dads bringing their sons rather than groups of lads out to have a bit of a stupid time. We don't tend to get much trouble.*

The thriving Sunday Market takes place in a large yard alongside the Tobacco Factory. 'It's definitely getting busier on North Street, even on a Sunday,' says Anna. 'It's amazing the amount of people walking around because of the Market. It depends on the weather: if it's gloomy, we're busy; if it's sunny, the Market's busy.' George Ferguson sums up the Tobacco Factory as follows: 'It's about community; it's about south Bristol's regeneration; it's about food, theatre, conversation, activity.'

# RALEIGH ROAD TO LIME ROAD 276-268

**T**he building on the opposite corner of Raleigh Road from the Tobacco Factory was built for the National Provincial and Union Bank. The bank originally had premises further along North Street (234), but by 1921 had moved to this location, still in use as a bank, now a branch of NatWest.

Jill Sims recalls working there:

*I was on the counter and later in customer services. On New Year's Eve we'd work really late, doing ledgers. We used the upstairs as a staff kitchen [and] we were allowed to use the canteen in Wills. There were lots of machines that processed cheques.*

*The manager was in his office most of the day – he didn't come out and get involved. Customers used to come and see him.*

Beyond the entrance alongside the bank is a rank of four shops, built c1910, the first of which is a long-established newsagents, currently Royston Garden

The west end of North Street, 2013. The Tobacco Factory, with Aldi to its left, dominates the view. Lower left is St Francis's Church and the remaining buildings of the brewery. To the right of the photo is the Victorian and Edwardian development of Southville, its roads punctuating North Street to create ranks of around eight shops

News (**see 274**). Next door (272), a branch of the Cats' Protection League charity, was originally a tobacconists, then a milliners from the 1930s to the 60s. The Salon, ladies' hairdresser (270), was a drapers shop from the 1920s till the 1970s, run by sisters Frances and Muriel Stringer: 'You could get everything there, needles, threads, knicker elastic, all sorts of things – anything that ladies needed', recalls Esme Davidson who left Merrywood School 'one Friday in July 1937 and started work on the [following] Monday at Stringer's. I worked sixty hours a week for the sum of 6/- (30p).' When the Stringers retired, the shop continued in the same business, trading as Fabrics.

Gilbert Woffenden ran his bakery at number 268 from its construction until the 1950s. Joan Nurmeleht, now in her 80s and still working in North Street, remembers serving in Woffenden's:

*They baked all the bread and rolls*

*and sold it in the shop. This was in about 1932. He was German and used to get quite a lot of flak. We had brass rods hanging from the windows and on Saturdays I had to polish them and scrub the bake house floor. I was about 14 or 15 then. Mr and Mrs Woffenden, two older ladies and me used to work there. I left there and went to work at Wills.*

Phyllis Neale also has fond memories of Woffenden's: 'Beautiful cakes! We never saw cakes like it before and us kids would stand looking through the window. They were class.' Sheila Williams also remembers how 'they used to do fritters. Mum used to go in and buy them and she would spread them with jam. They were like pancakes, the size of a tea plate!' However, Mervyn Southway is less romantic: 'They used to keep their cakes in the window and you used to see all the wasps around the cakes, but people didn't take any notice.' After Woffenden's, the shop continued as a bakers, Robbins, until the late 1960s. It is now the Ashton office of CJ Hole, estate agents.

Photographed from the middle of the road, near the current NatWest bank by Raleigh Road, looking east. Left, Scotts Stores (266) on the corner of Lime Road is offering London Stout & Ales, and on the right is Raleigh Road Post Office (271) next to Charles Treleaven's Piano shop (269). Only the children have time to pose. The shops date this c1911-1929

(Right) Perhaps a showery summer's day, with enough time between vehicles (and horses) for a pose at the junction of Raleigh Road and North Street c1923-1930. Note the corner of the Plaza cinema on the right, and the private bridge that remained a feature of Raleigh Road until the demolition of the tobacco factories. (Left) In 2014, around ninety years later, no-one poses for the camera

# 274 SIMS, NEWSAGENTS

(NOW ROYSTON GARDEN NEWS, NEWSAGENT)

👉 **Royston Garden News is still referred to by many local people as 'Sims' after its first owner John Sims, 'a tall man with a shock of black hair', recalls Peter Brimble.** Roy Pullin also remembers the shop:

*In the '40s it was very busy. I remember it was common to see boys waiting around for delivery of the evening edition of the papers so their newspaper rounds could be made up. One thing I particularly remember was that the newsagent used to sell foreign stamps. They had sheets of 'Approvals' each consisting of thirty or so stamps individually marked with their price. You were allowed to look through the sheets at your leisure deciding which stamp you would buy for your album. It was then taken off with a pair of tweezers and placed in a little paper bag – all for just a couple of coppers!*

From 1971 until 1995 the shop was run by Andrew and Dorothy Hamer:

*People used to call us 'Mr and Mrs Sims' but we didn't mind. The name was on the doorstep and we didn't want to change it. We'd never run a newsagents before, we were as green as grass. Of course you learn the hard way. I was a printer in Bolton*

Andrew Hamer outside his shop (274) in 1980, the window full of toys and adverts for cigarettes

*but I could see there was no future in printing so we bought a book called How to Run a Business which said that a newsagents was quite good to run – hard work but a lot of common sense.*

*We sold newspapers, sweets, a lot of toys and cigarettes of course – 60p for twenty Lambert and Butler in those days. When cigarettes went to £1, BBC 'Points West' interviewed me and I said 'Once cigarettes hit the pound*

*barrier you'll see the market collapse!' Although we sold a tremendous amount we didn't make a lot out of cigarettes. Even if we sold them at a loss, we couldn't be cheaper than supermarkets. Sweets and chocolate were our big money-makers. We used to buy a vast amount of chocolate which was packed in 'outers' of 40 bars. We bought 200 'outers' of Cadburys Dairy Milk at a time and could do offers because Cadbury's*

Raleigh Road to Lime Street, 2013

Sims newsagents soon after the Hamers took over the shop in the early 1970s. Note the cigarette machines on the pavement

and Rowntree's used to give us good terms. [For cigarettes] a rep would come from Wills' and we'd order from him. They were very strict about payments: you had to have your cheque ready. We used to do quite well with cards – Gordon Fraser, Classic. You went to the shows in January to order for Christmas. We used to go to the toy fair in Brighton. We stocked a lot of Dinkie and Corgi cars, hundreds of them!

Like other shopkeepers along North Street in the 1960s and early 70s, the Hamers relied on workers from the nearby Wills' factory for steady trade:

We were busy in the morning and then lunchtime. The 'Wills' Girls' were very generous. At Christmas they used to come in the shop and buy lots of games to give away for charity. If one of the Girls was pregnant they used to club together and buy her everything.

Due to the success of the business, the Hamers needed to employ assistants. 'Flo Jenkins, who lived in Headley Park, was with us, as was Lily White and Aileen Gent. She was very loyal, came to work for us about four months and stayed for about twenty years. The newspapers were delivered very early in the morning and we had a spate of somebody cutting the string on the bundles of papers and helping himself. The police staked it out but the thief must have seen them and never took any again.'

Lin Cox and her brother Kevin remember visiting Sims as children: 'There was a man came to Sims one Saturday morning to teach you to yo-yo. I don't know if he was from the company who sold yo-yos, but he was very good and used to make his yo-yo do the butterfly.'

The introduction of the National Lottery in 1994 added pressure on smaller shops where ticket terminals were located. 'It was hard work when the Lottery came in – Fridays and Saturdays were manic.' The Hamers decided to call it a day and retired.

# LIME ROAD TO GATHORNE ROAD 266-252

**T**his parade of eight shops was completed c1907, six of them being three-storey buildings in red brick with elegant stone banding. Since the day they opened, these shops have sold a range of commodities including groceries, footwear, animal feed, fruit and vegetables, as well as coal and spectacles.

The shop (266) on the corner of Lime Road, currently McColl's, a 'convenience store', has been in continuous use as a food shop for over a hundred years. It started life as Scott's Stores, later becoming the butchery department

of the nearby Co-op, as June Hodge recalls:

*We used to buy 'milk checks' in there – little plastic discs. Instead of putting money out on the step for milk you'd put milk checks. In those days you had a dividend number and you'd give your number when you bought anything in there and at the end of the year Mum would get her 'divi'.*

Over the years, the next two premises, now the Southville Deli (**see 262-260**), have sold a variety of goods. Number 258 started life as a William Mills, boot shop, and carried on selling footwear until the late 1950s

Lime Road to Gathorne Road, 2013. The oldest shops in this rank are those furthest right; North Street was developed westwards (from right to left) towards the tobacco factories.

when the RiteWear shop (as it was by then) became a hairdressers, 'Richard of London'. No doubt the name was intended to create a sophisticated image for clients in 'The Swinging Sixties', matched by Maison Francis further along the road (**see 146**).

Opening first as a newsagent, number 256 later became the office of the Bedminster Coal Supply Company. After a period as a 'gown specialist' in the

1940s and early 50s, the shop was run for over 20 years as Hall's Hardware.

Sidney Collins (254) sold animal feed, but is remembered for the chickens on display in the shop window. '[He] sold corn from sacks – the smell as you went in from all the different feed – you can't imagine', recall Bernard and Alma Chalmers. 'In the window he had day-old chicks and we used to peer in. People used to keep chickens in their back gardens and fed them on corn. A lot of people kept pigeons as well.'

Like many families during the Second World War, Glyn Williams' parents kept hens for both eggs and meat and his regular task was 'to go to Collins and get pearl barley to feed the chickens.' Ken and Muriel Eley also recall the window display: 'You could buy chickens there and they had a hand-drawn picture of a chicken pulling an elephant – "buy chickens as strong as elephants!"' Clive Green is certain that 'all children used to have a chicken in a shoe box.' However, not all the local traders were keen on having an animal feed shop close by, as Sylvia Sleeman remembers: 'They had a plague of mice or rats at one stage. My dad [Percy Clark, manager of Clark's Pies on the opposite side of North Street, **see 259**] was worried to death in case they came into our shop!' Sidney Collins continued trading until the 1960s. In recent years, the shop sold fitted kitchens ('Think Kitchens') and is now one of a row of three charity shops, Tenovus, St Peter's, and Children's Hospice South West .

The last shop (252) in the rank started life as a greengrocers. Stuart Amesbury recalls the family business, run by his parents and grandparents: 'I

At Scott's, on the corner of Lime Road, gooseberry jam is 7d for a 2lb jar, and Lion Tea is advertised as being a 'Power of Strength'. In the window are framed photographs of shops, probably their other branches. To the right is Dennings the optician. Next door-but-one is the Reliance Restaurant (260), marked with an X on this postcard, perhaps to show where the sender had drunk some 'excellent Fry's cocoa'. Mill's boot shop, (258, which later became RiteWear) sports a hanging illuminated globe, as do several other shops. The businesses date this photo to around the mid-1920s.

Scott's Stores (266) after closing time. Probably c1920s

lived through my childhood at the North Street premises. Before retiring, my grandparents also ran a shop in East Street, Bedminster. My parents retired in the late 1970s.' The Amesbury' shop is also remembered by Jill Sims: 'Mrs Amesbury did our wedding flowers.' The shop is now Parsons Bakery.

The Salvation Army Band plays Christmas carols outside 266 North Street, 2013

# 260-262 SOUTHVILLE DELI

👉 **In the 1920s, Mrs Edith Jenkins ran a pork butchers at number 262, while next door were 'refreshment rooms' run by a Miss Richards.** Local residents Peggy Triggle and Phyllis Neale remember both shops were later run by the Jenkins family. Phyllis recalls: 'Mrs Jenkins cooked hams and if you wanted to treat yourself you'd get your ham there. When her son came home after the war she bought the café next door.'

Peggy Triggle became a regular customer when the shop, run by Mrs Jenkins' son, Melville, switched to selling ladies' clothes: 'Lovely clothes – lingerie. I can remember buying a lovely dress in there, it was blue and white. I got off the bus on Redcliff Hill and a man said to me "You look lovely in that." I didn't know him from Adam!' Later on, the ladies' clothes shop expanded to selling wool and at some point the two premises were knocked through, trading as Rite Wools. This firm also had shops in Gloucester Road and Downend, but by 1996 the company had been wound-up. Peggy Triggle, like several other people, recalls the variety and quality of goods available in North Street in the 1950s: 'You could do all your Christmas shopping in [there]. It

L to R: Southville Deli proprietor Paul Wick with staff Guy Thomas and Michael Gambriel. 2014

was very nicely done, Jenkins was a very nice shop where you could buy tights and lots of lovely wools. People knitted a lot in those days. You could buy presents in there and you got quality.'

For a time, number 260 was the Reliance Café, then becoming the Four Leaf Clover café, probably the same one remembered by Graham Hopewell and Barbara Thorn as 'Mrs Burrell's, where people from Wills' used to go for lunch [it was so busy you] couldn't get a seat.'

In 2001, Paul Wick, one of North Street's more recent entrepreneurs, opened the Southville Deli in number 260. Realising there was a gap in the market, Paul picked up ideas for the kind of business he wanted to run by visiting similar shops elsewhere. The result was a mixture of a whole-food shop and a deli. At the start, Paul worked six days a week on his own until the business got going and he could employ a part-timer:

*Initially we didn't sell bread or sandwiches. These later went on to become big components in the business. In expanding my range, I relied on customers coming in and saying 'Can you get this?' – and we did. Then of course that person kept coming back to buy an everyday item like milk and they'd pick up something else and that's how the business grew. I have rarely said we won't or don't stock that. If it can easily be got in a supermarket, then we tend not to, but otherwise we are open to most requests.*

After a year, Paul realised that the wide pavement in front of the shop could be utilised and then started selling drinks and snacks. By 2008, Paul needed more room for his expanding range, so knocked through to the adjoining shop. The type of customers varies through the week:

*It's not quite so hip and trendy as other people paint it. Monday to Friday our customers included Wills'* pensioners [who] treat themselves here, and lots of parents with young children. Then at the weekend we get more couples shopping together, or just visiting the street for a bit of a jolly. What some call 'the old Bedminster characters' who I was very fond of, they've largely died out.

Like other traders along North Street, Paul had concerns when new supermarkets opened nearby, but in practice he has found that they have attracted more people to the street: 'I think there are more people on the pavement dapping in and out of the other shops as well.' Paul's is clear about why his business has been so successful:

It's quite a difficult street to be a specialist [shop] because you constantly need to attract someone through the door. We also have the card shop over the road (Cardiac, **see 253**). If it just sold cards [that could be difficult], but it is sweets as well, so there are a few different reasons for people to walk in. We have a good butcher and veg shop nearby and we have made a triangle of good places to shop for everyday stuff. If we were stood alone we wouldn't be half as successful as that. We have to keep on growing or someone else will roll up and do it. You've always got to look over your shoulder as well.

Paul is confident that North Street will continue to thrive and is determined his own business will prosper and expand.

# CHAPTER 20
# GATHORNE ROAD TO EXETER ROAD 250-236

Taken from upstairs at Clark's Pies (259) c1955. The Reliance Cafe (260, now Southville Deli) seen in the 1920s photo is still in business. Sydney Collins (254) is selling Spratts dog food, and the butcher W Lye (250, now Rare Meat Butchers) has a prominent sign on the corner of Gathorne Road. The Brooke Bond tea van is likely to have picked up its load locally, from the factory in Redcliffe Backs

t the start of the twentieth century, this section of North Street was still very much a lane with barely a handful of buildings. By 1903, Gathorne and Raleigh roads had been built, followed by Lime, Exeter and Greville roads in 1910, thereby creating four neat ranks of shops, among which were two butchers, a boot maker, refreshment rooms, a chemist, two grocers and a stationers.

A century on and butchers shops occupy the same premises, as does a chemists. Sheila Williams remembers one of the shops in the 1950s selling tasty take-away food: 'We used to go from Guides on a Friday night with a jug to get faggots and peas – the whole mix in the jug – and take it home for supper.'

The stationers (240) was originally run by Albert Coles and by the mid-1950s, Cyril Williams, an ex-

85

NORTH ST, ASHTON, BRISTOL.

The west end of North Street, with George Frederick Knowles' grocers on the corner of Exeter Road (236, currently Strada cycles). Far left is Gittins (242). James Nelson's butchers is probably a branch of the large national chain. In the distance on the brow of the hill is the Hen and Chicken. Undated, but probably c1910

1928 White Funnel brochure. Knowles supplied provisions for the company.

professional footballer who played for Bristol City Football Club was the manager. According to Dave Russell, Williams continued to take a keen interest in the fortunes of his old club and Brian Sleeman recalls: 'You'd wait there for the football papers to come out on a Saturday night – *The Pink'un* and *The Green'un* – and if The City had lost there would be quite a lot of banter. He ran the shop with his brother Les.' Frank Phillips remembers 'buying some football boots here in 1969. They were red and were autographed "Gordon Banks World Cup Winner." They were the best football boots I ever had.' Valerie Pearce recalls the 1956/57 season: 'If they played away on the weekend he'd get a

sheet of cardboard and he'd get photos from the paper and stick them on and put it in the window so you'd be able to see the match pictures. It was like Match of the Day. He sold a few sporting bits and pieces as well.'

The shop (236) on the corner of Exeter Road was a grocers for over 60 years, including a branch of the local Knowles chain (**see 144**). By the late 1940s, it was trading as Ross's. Jill Sims, who lived over the road, remembers that 'Mr Pastry [Richard Hearne, the popular comedian who had a show on BBC television] ran a promotion at Ross's.' The shop is now Strada, a well-regarded independent bike shop.

Knowles advertisement in the 1928 White Funnel brochure. George Frederick Knowles operated the North Street branch of his grocery business from number 236.

20

GATHORNE ROAD TO EXETER ROAD | 250-236

# 250 BOB WHERLOCK, BUTCHERS

(NOW RARE MEATS)

 **This shop has been in continuous use as a butchers, run first by the Clarke Brothers.** By 1921 it was trading as Henry Arthur Lye, and continued under this name until taken over by Bob Wherlock in 1975. Lye's was another popular destination for Wills' workers, as Alma Chalmers testifies: 'The Girls chased up to Lye's in their lunchtime and queued for their meat. Then they'd chase across the road to Young's or Amesbury's for their greens for that night, all in an hour!' Peggy Triggle describes Lye's home-delivery service before the Second World War: 'Grandmother did all the ordering. They came to the house, you never went to the shop. A boy would come on a bicycle and he'd come to the door and Grandma would say"I'll have chops tomorrow". He'd deliver it the next day and she'd give him another list and so on.'

Wherlock's was famous for its wonderful displays of meats of every description, as well as the famous 'Southville Sizzler' sausage, the lengthy queues at Christmas and the cheery greeting which awaited every customer from Bob and his team. Bob tells his story:

*I had a shop previously in Yate.*

*Ted and Doris Lye were retiring so I arranged to go there for a month before I took the business on to get to know the customers. I wanted to change it completely, as Ted's idea of running the shop and mine were completely different. We took the shop on in November 1975 when I was 35. By Christmas, my wife, Di, was helping me. When we first started, the majority of workers from Wills' had gone so we didn't have the rush. Even still, we were always busy. In the early days my dad used to help me. He wasn't a butcher but he used to get out the back and scrub the chitterlings off. My brother, who was also a butcher, used to help out. Then I advertised the job and Frank Stait arrived. He was with me for thirty-two years and Ken Butcher for about twenty-eight.*

The shop was noted for selling Aberdeen Angus beef and displayed the Scotland flag above the door.

*We also specialised in chitterlings and we made our own sausages. There used to be about nine butchers on North Street. There was Dennis Butt, Ron Sage, and the Co-op. Fine Fare had a butcher's counter, and Jack Hedges was a very good butcher. On down North Street towards Cannon Street there were about another four. I was always friendly with them all. If we ran out of anything we'd borrow pieces of meat. We had a seat in the shop so at least two people could sit and we had cups of tea and biscuits and things for the*

Bob Wherlock holding a tray of his famous 'Southville Sizzlers'. Frank Stait (with glasses) and Ken Butcher

*kids. We always had large queues at Christmas. By the time they came into the shop they'd been chatting to each other.*

Will Holland worked on Saturdays as 'butcher's boy' at the shop from 1993 to 1997: 'When I got to work at 6.30am, Bob, Frank and Ken were already there. I used to weigh the joints and write out the price tickets, but the worst job was getting the ham hocks out of the boiler. I had to reach into the jelly with my arm and in winter it was freezing!'

The butchering tradition has continued with the opening of Rare, voted Bristol's best butcher in the Good Food Awards in 2014. The smells of cooking from its giant pavement barbeque, serving black pudding and sausages in baps, draws customers every Friday and Saturday.

# 248 HEALTH UNLIMITED

Penny Barnett, shop manager, Health Unlimited, 2013

👉 **For more than half a century, boots and shoes were sold here, but in 2002 it 'reopened' as Health Unlimited.**
Manager Penny Barnett explains the business approach:

*We do a bit of everything. People come in and buy a card, or a present for a friend they are going to meet for coffee. They can buy their vitamins and toys for their children, and we even sell stamps! [We have] regulars who have been coming since the beginning, and then you get a lot of newer families with young children. Some people come in not sure what they want: they just know that there could be something here that might help them, so you have to figure out what they may need for their health. You get people who have heard about certain products passed down through the generations, such as molasses or liquorice. Other people really know their stuff and are devoted to health. Some people come in when they have been to the doctor's and been advised to take something quite life-changing, such as steroids, and they come in here to find an alternative.*

Penny describes her shop as 'a very welcoming place, the staff bring a nurturing side to the street. We like to give our knowledge and pass that on, to give people positivity, thinking about their health and helping themselves.' The shop has a good relationship with the nearby chemists: 'They sometimes send people to us if they are looking for homeopathy', says Penny, 'and sometimes we advise people to go to them.' Penny feels there is definitely a community in the street and some of the new shops will bring in more customers. It feels to her that a change is slowly happening: 'It will make it more like an everyday high street, and people will have less need to go into the Centre.'

# 246 BERNARD HUNTER & BRISTOL CINE

 **If you want to buy a cine camera, a second-hand Leica, or have your grandparents' wedding movie digitised, then Bernard Hunter is the place to go.**
The shop has been selling photographic equipment since 1990 and the manager is Andrew Nicholls. In 1977, Andrew, a former industrial photographer, purchased the Bernard Hunter shop in West Street. Business boomed and

Andrew Nicholls in 2014 with an original Nikon F. Andrew explains that it was 'Introduced in 1959 as the company's first SLR, and became the first to be widely adopted by professional photographers'

Andrew began searching for larger premises, moving to North Street in 1990 into a shop with an illustrious past as Photoradio, formerly one of two adjoining shops established by Dr Hedley Price.

Developing and printing were originally done in a darkroom upstairs, but this had become redundant by the time Andrew Nicholls took over, because the Kodak film processing service was 'so swift and reliable you could bring in a film by 10am and it would be ready to pick up by 4pm!' A regular customer in those days was Cameron Balloons and as the balloon crew drove past the shop from an early morning test flight in Ashton Court with photos of a new balloon, they would drop the film off and the prints would be back by the afternoon.

Andrew says that his business now caters for a niche market, but when he started he was selling the type of products which would have been found in any other photographic shop. He was quick to respond to specialist interest by buying a mail order cine equipment company and was still selling new cine cameras as recently as 1990. Although sales of equipment from the shop are relatively low, Andrew has a thriving internet business. He sells items that might have hung about 'for thirty five years and we put them on the "web" and the ink doesn't even dry!' Andrew agrees that his shop 'is the last of a species' and is convinced that money can no longer be made by selling new cameras in the high street. He gets lots of customers referred by other shops: 'We don't do that – try Bernard Hunter in Bedminster.' As customers enter one of the last independent photographic shops in the region and squeeze their way through the aisle of camera bags, 35mm SLRs, reels of cine film, developing tanks and film splicers, they encounter one of the most knowledgeable photographic dealers in the South West.

Andrew Nicholls, proprietor of Bernard Hunter, 2014

# 246 HEDLEY PRICE PHOTORADIO
(NOW BERNARD HUNTER)

**Mary Barnes went to work for the Hedley Price family in 1951, later running the business with Ken Haynes:**

Dr Price had four chemist shops – in Bishopsworth, West Street and 10 and 244 North Street – as well as the radio shop. Mr Price junior took on [numbers] 244 and 246. He was a doctor like his father. Mr Dumbleton was the manager of the chemists and Mr Wring was the manager in the radio shop. He delivered an Alba Consul radio, fairly big with dials on the front, to my father and I said I wanted a job. I was only about eight at the time! Later on, when I was 16 or 17 I met Mr Wring who told me there was a

job going so I went as an assistant in the radio shop.

We sold cameras, films, radios – no TVs in those days – all kinds of electrical equipment, Dinky Toys, Hornby train sets. There was an interconnecting door for the staff but it was two separate shops for the customers. At the back was the darkroom where we used to develop films. Ken Haynes did all the radio repairs upstairs. We had three photographers who did the weddings, Don Loader, Terry Cleaves and David

Hedley Price's photographic shop (246), now Bernard Hunter. 'Price's Perfect Prints Please' is just one of the many slogans which adorned the company's shop windows and the 1933 catalogue in which this photo was featured

Hedley Price Photoradio c1980. L to R: Mary Barnes; Ken Haynes; George Whitlock. The display shelves with illuminated Perspex titles such as Batteries and Films have been retained, as can be seen in the photo of current owner Andrew Nicholls

Evans. I remember battery-mains radios coming in and then the first televisions. You couldn't walk on the pavements when the Wills' people turned out and we all used to rub our hands with glee when they got their bonuses! When the Cup Final was on we had a television in the shop window and the customers used to come and sit and watch it. I have very many happy memories of working there and in the end, took it over. We finished in 1990 and put up a notice saying 'Ken and Mary wish to thank all customers and friends for gifts, cards and good wishes.'

Alma Chalmers remembers the shop soon after the war:

*The radio shop went on to sell televisions when they first came out. They did our wedding photographs, made up books with the photos. They*

took a photograph of me before colour and my Mum said 'I don't want it, look at the colour of her socks!' They looked grey and it was 'Persil white' for Mum, so Mr Wring worked on it and made my socks look white!

As a child in the 1960s, Steve Williamson also recalls the Hedley Price shops:

*My mother knew all the people [who worked there]. My train set came from Photoradio and was the one in the window, so no doubt Mum and Dad got it slightly cheaper. It didn't last very long but they did repair it. They also sold a few other toys because the day I took my 'eleven plus' in 1962, my father took me up and bought me three model fire engines 'cos I was mad keen on fire engines.*

# 244 HEDLEY PRICE, CHEMISTS
(NOW LLOYD'S PHARMACY, CHEMISTS)

**The firm of Hedley Price began in 1899 with a pharmacy at 252 North Street and expanded rapidly, by 1901 moving to larger premises (244), then opening a shop in nearby West Street in 1906.** In 1927, 246 North Street opened for 'photographic and Radio activities'. Frank Phillips remembers the latter shop as his father, Laurie, was the dispenser there and his step mother, Betty, also worked in the shop:

*He used to mix up his own medicines. If you had a chesty cough he used to make up a cough mixture. It was*

Ernest Dumbleton's retirement c1975. L to R: May Nobbs, Mrs Dumbleton, Mr Dumbleton, Dr Godfrey Price

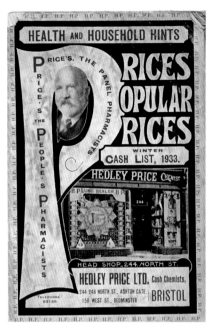

1933 winter catalogue, showing 244 North Street. The window is advertising the HP Lung Healer

*referred to as 'Laurie's Mixture'. He never told anyone what was in the medicine and took the secret to his grave. My father used to sometimes do the wedding photos. In 1951 Festival of Britain there was a crown made out of flowers on the Centre in town and some photos in black and white. My mother did some of the tinting of the photos to put some colour into them and she did the flowers on the picture of the crown.*

# 242 SMITH & HOPEWELL AND GITTINS
(NOW MEDITERRANEAN, BAR/RESTAURANT)

**The Gittins family started trading in the early 1900s, running a much-respected grocers for over sixty years.** Like many shops of the period, it offered a home delivery service, as Janet Steele recalls: 'They used to send somebody round to your house and take your order, then deliver it, then the next week you would pay for the order. When we moved down to Tickenham, Mr Gittins still delivered to us – all the way to Tickenham!' Alma Chalmers has clear memories of shopping in Gittins' during the Second World War. 'There was a man who sliced the bacon on the machine to the thickness that you wanted. His name was Mr Field and he was the superintendent from the Sunday School. He had a big smiley face. He also weighed out the sugar and the butter exactly because it was on ration, then wrapped it in greaseproof.'

The Gittins business continued until 1967, when brother and sister Graham Hopewell and Barbara Thorn took over the shop. They had lived with their family above Playfair's shoe shop, 248 North Street from 1938, and both went into the grocery trade. On leaving school at 14, Graham went to work in the grocery department of the Co-op on Chessell Street. Barbara also joined the Co-op staff at their North Street branch (264-266) 'because in those days they didn't allow members of the same family in the same department.' As fellow members of the Bristol and West Grocers' Association they met Bill Gittin, and eventually took over his shop as Graham describes:

*I changed the shop into semi self-service after I took it over. The Smith part of the name was my partner, Fred*

**91**

Smith. Between the two shops we had about fourteen members of staff, mostly part-time. We worked five and a half days a week and sold groceries and cooked meats, tinned goods, bacon, bread, milk. I can remember we used to order a side of bacon which you had to bone and roll and work out your profit. When Wills' were still down the road we'd have a queue right outside the door. I used to sell about 400 tins of biscuits at Christmas! We'd have to be at the North Street shop by 6.30am because the baker and milkman would be waiting. We opened at 7am and closed at 5.30pm, then when the staff had gone home we'd probably be there for another couple of hours cashing up and re-stocking the shelves. After we started, Fine Fare came and the Home & Colonial. Ross's were on the corner of Exeter Road and the Co-op too. Most of us all got on very well.

Smith and Hopewell also offered a home delivery service. Once the new estates of Withywood and Hartcliffe were built in the mid-1950s, many people who had moved there from Ashton and Bedminster continued to use Smith and Hopewell for their groceries: 'We took the best part of a hundred orders a week from Withywood and Hartcliffe and we had a dedicated delivery van and driver, going out on Monday and Tuesday collecting orders around the estates. Then we'd make them all up and deliver on Thursdays and Fridays.' Graham and Barbara retired in April 1997, by which time Barbara had worked in shops on North Street for 55 years.

# 238 D R BUTT, BUTCHERS

 **Prior to being owned by Dennis Butt, this butchers was run by Ernest Burgess.** A local resident remembers his father working in Mr Burgess's slaughterhouse:

*Dad used to bring the chitterlings home which he would clean and boil. They were very tasty. He was also given the cows' udders which were put in the pram wrapped in a white sheet and we used to have to take them to a little shop in Cathay, Redcliffe, where they used to cook and sell them.*

David Casely has a particular reason to remember Mr Burgess:

*On Christmas Day 1941, seven days after my father had been killed, my mother and I walked to my grandparents' house for dinner. On the way, I was told they had only managed to obtain a small rabbit for our Christmas dinner, but on arrival the smell of a roast turkey greeted us and on the table was a plum pudding and a Christmas cake! The turkey had been given to my grandmother by Burgess' the North Street butchers, the pudding and cake had been donated by Wintle's the grocers, who used to be on the corner of Agate Street.*

Nowadays the shop is managed by Harold Coleman, known to regular customers as 'H'. His assistant is Scott Maxwell.

*I've been here about eight years, but I first started working for Dennis Butt in 1964, aged fourteen, as Saturday boy. Monday afternoons I made the faggots*

Harold Coleman, known to regular customers as 'H', in Butt's butchers, 238 North Street

Small game at Butt's, 238 North Street

*and Wednesday afternoons the dripping. I'd come in on Sunday morning to clean the fridge out and got an extra ten shillings. There was a lot of customers then because of Wills'. The place was packed dinner time and evenings. Den*

*Butt had four staff in the shops then because it was so busy. There were trays of chitterling and gammon hocks in the window. The chitterling was delivered warm from Britton's, put in the window from 11.30 and then Wills' came out and that was it – gone!*

*I start at 5.30am five days a week, 5am on Saturday, and finish about 5.30pm. We cook our own beef, turkey, pork and gammon hocks in the ovens overnight so it's ready when I come in at 5.30am. The older cuts of meat like brisket of beef on the bone are coming back into fashion. I think television chefs have a lot to answer for. I had a chap come in the other day asking for an oxtail to be boned out and I said 'Goodbye!' I've never boned an oxtail so I wouldn't know how to start. Lamb shanks used to be cheap but they're so expensive now I'd have to sell them for £5 each. We've just started doing our own sausages again. I used to buy mine from a chap in Gloucester but he started getting expensive.*

*In summer we do the barbeque stuff – kebabs, different flavours. I put a few in the window and people come and want some more so I make them out the back. Someone might come in and say can you do me £25 or £50 worth of barbeque stuff so I stay until eight or nine at night making it because they want it early the next day. It's on the go all the time and we have a few orders as well for local restaurants. I don't want to sound big-headed but I take a pride in my work.*

# CHAPTER 21

# EXETER ROAD TO GREVILLE ROAD 234-220

his rank of eight, three storey shops was built in 1899.

Several of the shops have provided the same service for many decades: 234 was a chemists for over fifty years, and the shop now Denny's Bakery has been a bakers since it was built.

## 234 HODDER'S, CHEMISTS
(NOW CURTIS AND BELL, CAFÉ)

 **The shop on the corner of Exeter Road opened as Mrs Kemp's china, glass and stationery dealer, but by 1921 it had become Henry Hodder & Co, chemist and druggists.** The firm traded for nearly fifty years until it was taken over and became a branch of Weston (Chemists) Ltd. Lin Cox started working as a pharmaceutical technician there when she was sixteen:

*When I went there in 1970 it was all wooden fittings behind the counter with little drawers with brass handles from the time it was Hodder's. One job I had to do was to clean the brass handles. Behind the counter were sliding doors and above that it was all mirror-back shelving which had to be cleaned on a regular basis as well. The heating was still done by gas dome things. We had a very big glass-fronted floor unit which went the length of the shop. In those days you had to serve people properly, so you had to get everything out of the drawers and lay them out on the counter for the customers to see. At the back of the dispensary were glass cupboards where all the perfumes were kept.*

*Mr Leslie Moreton-Webb was the pharmacist and he used to live above the shop. The pharmacy section was on the back and then you had another little room which was the stockroom. You had to hand-write all the labels, then it progressed to typewriter. You had to make sure all the labels were straight.*

Number 234, one of only a few North Street buildings declaring its date

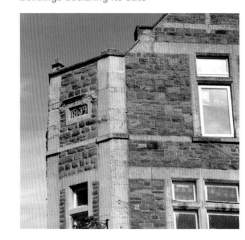

93

*We used to sell gas soda streams as well. I started off doing my training there – had to work for a year before they put me forward to do the training which was for three years day-release. I went to the college in Ashley Down which was quite a trek. College started at 9.00am so I had to leave at 7.30, get to Redcliffe Hill then on to Ashley Down and I used to get home about 7.30pm.*

During the thirty years that Lin worked there, the shop changed hands several times, at one time being a branch of Spracket's, Grove Hart and finally Lloyd's Pharmacy. Since 2000, the premises has been occupied by a number of different businesses: Blockbuster Videos, Moviebank (DVD rental) and now Curtis and Bell, tearooms.

# 228 IVORY FLOWERS & ZARA'S CHOCOLATES

 **Xanthe Ivory set up her business in 2011, selling flowers from the entrance lobby of the Tobacco Factory, but had ambitions to move into a shop which she did in 2013, moving into 228 North Street which she shares with chocolatier, Zara Narracott.** Xanthe is passionate about flowers and her job:

*It is a lot harder than I thought it was going to be, but I don't want to do anything else. Say we've got a wedding – we do the shop here and then go and do the wedding. We've been known to be up till midnight for the wedding the next day. You just do it all the time,*

# 226 LUTON AND SONS, BAKERS
(NOW DENYS, BAKERS)

**In the 1960s and 70s, Luton's was the second largest independent bakery in Bristol, with shops throughout the city.** Gordon Luton, grandson of Edward Luton who founded the company, tells its story:

*Edward Luton started the bakery business in 1901. He was a farm labourer's son from Winterbourne, born in 1869 I think. When he was nineteen and having tried other jobs, he went to work for the village baker and the first morning he was there he thought 'This is it, I'm going to be a baker.' His aunt lent him £100 to buy a small bakery in Midland Road, with his fiancée, Minnie Upton, in 1893. To begin with he made the bread himself and pushed it around St Phillips on a barrow, selling it to small shops.*

In order to expand his business, Edward bought a horse but it died the following day. This tragedy, combined with the fluctuating price of flour and Edward's lack of experience, resulted in bankruptcy. Determined to start afresh, Edward rented premises in the Pithay area of Broadmead because it was close enough to a mill from which he could afford to buy one sack of flour at a time, and began baking again on a modest scale. Eventually he got himself out of trouble and bought a shop in

Barton Hill and when he had made enough money he began searching for a second shop. This was 226 North Street. 'He never looked back after that because down the road was the cigarette factory and in those days the workers didn't have cars. They walked to work past his shop and they'd call in to buy bread or cakes.'

Edward's family moved into the flat over the shop. After the hardship of the First World War things picked up and Edward bought another shop in East Street, Bedminster. He was a highly skilled baker, as Gordon explains:

*There used to be bread-making competitions around the country [and a] big one every year in London [run by] the Association of Master Bakers with different classes of breads like cottage and farmhouse and they'd get awarded points. In 1908 he got more points for his entries than anyone else and was declared Champion Baker of the United Kingdom. He was awarded over a thousand silver cups, medals and diplomas for his bread, cake and confectionery.*

After the Second World War, the firm continued to expand until it had over ten shops across Bristol. Bread and similar products were all baked in a factory in Smyth Road while all the cakes and confectionery were made at 226 North Street and distributed daily to the various branches. As well as the network of shops, Luton's operated a number of delivery rounds:

*In the early days we had horses*

One of Luton's loaf-shaped delivery vans. Harold King was the driver and he is recorded as saying that the photograph was not posed but taken by a stranger when he was delivering bread in Cumberland Road. The van apparently ended up on a farm and was used as a chicken house. Dated 1925. Harold's first job with Luton's was as a delivery boy with a horse and cart

AFB acted on behalf of a number of small, family-run bakeries, later moving to Avonmouth and changing its name to the Family Loaf Bakery. Gordon acknowledges that the factory couldn't produce bread of the same quality as that baked when Luton's operated as a truly independent firm, although they continued to make cakes and confectionery and cakes to the same high standard. Gordon eventually left the company, returning after his father's death in 1975 to take over. Although he had 'all sorts of idea to expand the company,' the recession in 1982-83 and fierce competition from supermarkets hit Luton's hard. 'We had a terrible year. We survived but knew we wouldn't survive another.' The Luton business was sold soon after to a company called Starbake.

Remembering Luton's as a child, one writer says: 'We used to go down the lane at the back and get up to no good. We used to "borrow" the fresh bread – the staff would be in [the bakery] playing cards – break it in half, take the middle out, over to Thompson's [chip shop], put six pennorth of chips in it and have a feast!'

A Luton's paper bag. Note the list of medals, the latest being at the 1935 Great Hertfordshire Show

and carts and the stables were in Smyth Road. We started off delivering door to door like milkmen. We had eighteen delivery rounds at one time, right across the city. Then we also supplied wholesale – Wills' factory canteen, BAC canteen, University halls of residence and hotel kitchens. We also did wedding cakes and we had a brilliant cake decorator.

The delivery rounds continued until the late 1950s when it became uneconomic and at the same time, the bakery business in general underwent a series of major changes: 'The big thing was sliced and wrapped bread. Big companies were formed to make sliced loaves and sell them to supermarkets. We tried to compete and bought a slicing and wrapping machine but we didn't have a freezer to put the bread in to chill and it was always a bit of a problem.' Luton's answer to competition from Mother's Pride and Sunblest was the 'Sylvita' loaf: 'My dad dreamed it up. The idea was it was bread with a silky texture and vitalising.'

Gordon joined the family business in 1948. To ward off the threat from the big companies, his father decided to start a firm called Associated Family Bakeries (AFB), initially based at the Luton's premises in Smyth Road.

you don't really stop, which is good 'cos it's fun. I get up at 5am and go to the market, and then I'll condition everything, then price it. There's a lot more labour goes into it than you see.

Xanthe lives locally and loves the area:

*Everyone smiles, everyone's friendly. People are much more behind you, especially older people, they say 'Hi'. People are more interested in you, and you being an independent shop. [They] are very much behind us: 'Good on you for doing it here.' It's full of characters, a really quintessential British place. There are a lot more happy mums around here getting nice bunches of flowers. Getting men out of trouble – maybe I'm keeping romance and some marriages alive! It brings a bit of colour to the road.*

## 224 BARBER'S EMPORIUM

**In the 1920s, there were fifteen family-run grocers in North Street, some with several shops.** National companies, including the Co-op and the Home & Colonial Stores, also operated shops here, the latter opening at 224 North Street towards the end of the decade. The Home & Colonial quickly became a firm favourite because of its quality and service, as Jack House describes:

*As a lad, I used to do errands for the lady who lived next door to us in Pearl*

Street and she would only have stuff purchased from the Home & Colonial. A weekly order – they always knew what I wanted before I asked for it. There were counters right round the side with people behind, a wonderful feel about the place. Everything was sparklingly clean.

Muriel Eley also recalls the Home & Colonial: 'We took our ration books there. I remember after the war when stuff was still on ration, we were going on holiday and he got Mum a tin of Penguin biscuits.' Local residents remember the shop and its manager, Mr Porter, during the 1960s and 70s: 'The goods were on the shelves or on the counter', recall Bernard and Alma Chalmers. 'You passed your shopping bag over to Mr Porter and he packed your shopping nice and neatly.' Mervyn Southway remembers that 'Mr Porter used to ride a bicycle to work and he always used to wear his bicycle clips in the shop.'

Ivan Carter worked as a relief manager for the company and he and his wife lived above the shop, moving there in 1969: [We] 'had a huge flat, on the first floor. Under the stairs was where the coal was kept – the poor coalman had to carry the coal up the stairs. It was a cold place but we had lovely coal fires.' Ivor learnt the trade from his father, who was manager of the Home & Colonial in Princess Victoria Street, Clifton. As relief manager, Ivor went round different branches including

Undated, this catalogue lists eleven branches in Bristol, including 224 North Street

Brian Billings at work in his Barber's Emporium, 224 North Street. 2013

the one in North Street. 'All the windows were dressed exactly the same. There was normally a fortnightly offer and they'd send you a picture of how it had to be dressed. Say you had a tinned fruit offer, you'd have to build up a stack a certain way and the posters had to be in the window a certain way.' The working week had many routines:

*At that time you only had two weeks' holiday a year, plus Bank Holidays. You worked between ten and twelve hours six days a week with half-day closing. The shops opened 8.30am to 5.30pm. Everything was in the window, meats, bacon, cheese. You had to prepare that. In the evening it would all go in the cold store. It would come up on a lorry and you'd unload. It was mainly 90lb cheeses – they were heavy! This used to come in crates and you'd leave the crates outside the shop at night and they would be gone next day. People would take it for firewood. You rang them up [to order], but a lot of the shops didn't have a phone. The North*

Street shop didn't have one, so we used the phone box opposite. The shop door was on the right, and to the left was the counter which was an L shape. On the right hand side would have been the big tins of biscuits which people could help themselves. It was mostly groceries, tea, sugar, bacon, cold meats and cheese. All the pulses and beans you had to weigh out into pounds.

The shop was still open, trading as Lipton's, when Ivor left in 1977, later becoming a branch of the Safeway chain.

In 2007, Brian Billings opened a men's hairdressers here, having started in the trade as an apprentice, working for four or five years in Gloucester Road. Brian, who grew up in Ashton, says he arrived in North Street at just the right time. He remembers that the area 'was miserable – half the shops boarded up – but I just got here as the whole street was coming up.' He has a steady stream of customers and works on his own but would like to train someone. Trade is a

lot brisker in the summer than winter: 'In the summer men get sweaty and decide it's time to have their hair chopped off. Hair is like loft insulation – you only want it in the winter!'

The Barber's Emporium is one of three barbers shops in North Street, but Brian says he has friendly relationships with them. 'Hair will continue to grow', says Brian, confident that 'men will continue to come to their local barbers for friendly banter, a chat about football, as well as a good trim.'

# 220 THOMAS ILES, GREENGROCER

(NOW ZAZU'S KITCHEN, BAR/RESTAURANT)

 **The shop which opened under this name in 1903, was originally run by Mervyn Southway's grandfather:**

*When he died my grandmother carried on with the business of*

*greengrocers. They didn't deal with the [Bristol wholesale] market, everything was fresh. They had a big nursery at Yatton – Elborough Nursery it was. Three of the sons worked the land and then transported the produce up to the shop. This would be when I was a boy about six or seven years old [in the 1930s]. In Iles, like all shops at the time, you were served. It was just family working there, they had a good selection of things and everything was completely seasonal. The nursery was vast. They had about half a dozen greenhouses and they grew tomatoes, apples, pears, potatoes, beans, strawberries, raspberries – anything that could be grown, they did! When my grandmother died one of my aunts, Mary Tanner, took over the shop [and] when the nursery was sold my aunt moved directly opposite into a shop which had sold ladies' dresses (211 R Cooper, costumier). She ran it as a greengrocers and her husband, Alex 'Harry' Tanner had the butchers next door.*

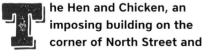

# GREVILLE ROAD TO UPPER SYDNEY STREET 218-178

**T**he Hen and Chicken, an imposing building on the corner of North Street and Greville Road, marks the beginning of one of the most varied stretches of North Street, which includes a pub, supermarket, a terrace of Edwardian shops, a row of Georgian houses **(mostly hidden behind single storey shop fronts), ending with a Victorian terrace, Carlton Villas.** North Street is frequently referred to as a 'street of two halves' and the roundabout just beyond the Hen and Chicken marks the divide.

Hen and Chicken with post-War restoration

# 210 THE HEN AND CHICKEN

👉 **This pub, referred to by locals as 'The Chick', is not only popular for a drink and a meal but is well-known in Bristol and beyond as a venue for stand-up comedy.** Phyllis Neale has clear recollections of the pub as it was before the Second World War: 'You used to be able to sit up on the roof in the garden of the Hen and Chicken.' Others have fond memories

of weddings and birthday parties here. The large window ledges at street level provided a popular vending place for *The Bristol Evening Post*.

The Hen and Chicken pub started life a short distance further along North Street in a double-fronted eighteenth century building on the site now occupied by the Co-op supermarket. This prominent position was opposite what was once the turnpike-gate to Luckwell Lane (now Luckwell Road). The original building was still standing in 1904, but around then the business moved

The Hen and Chicken, North Street, by Ernest Parkman. The picture is undated, but Parkman lived from 1856 – 1921. The scene shows what may have been an unrealistically neat and clean road, children and buildings. The cottage to the left is almost certainly George Hathway's shop (208) shown in the photograph in this chapter

Top: Hen and Chicken Hotel, Snack Bar and Restaurant gutted after a bombing raid. The shadow of boot maker George Hathway's demolished shop (208) can be seen beneath the advertisement on the side wall. The Belisha Beacon has lost its globe, but the sign to the swimming baths still clings to the tram pole. The two women wait beneath a sign 'S' for air-raid shelter, whilst a group stand and talk, where behind them the North Street sign has fallen into the rubble. The quality of the glass plate reveals that the inscription in the gable names the founder and the then family owner, reading "Jacob Clark 176(?)1 and Martin Clark 1904." Bottom: Ford cars stored at the rear of the bomb-damaged Hen and Chicken. In the rubble, which is behind the North Street frontage shown in the picture above, is the wreckage of a car.

The bombed pub seen from Greville Road. A handcart labelled Hen and Chicken Hotel stands in the cobbled yard, and a Shelter sign points towards North Street.

Photo taken possibly c1898 while the American Barnum and Bailey's Circus was on its European tour. Taken from near number 181 (currently Enid's Fish Bar), the crowds are out to watch the circus making its way to the fairground. The circus may have been in the fields that still bordered North Street (further along to the left in this picture), owned by the Hen and Chicken landlord. Middle-right is the original bay-windowed Hen and Chicken (see Parkman sketch.) Further right, out of the picture, is the current solicitors' building (192.) On the left, the trees are probably those in the garden of Luckwell House, whilst in the far distance is St Francis's Church. The horse-drawn tram is heading from Ashton Gate to Bristol Bridge

to a new public house which had been constructed on its current corner site. Anyone glancing up at the building might realise that the upper storeys have been rebuilt. This followed serious bomb damage in the air raids on Bristol in 1940-1. Vernon Windell recalls the popular story of 'Jim, a firewatcher, who recalls seeing a car blown onto the roof of the Hen and Chicken – lifted there in an explosion!' Apparently the car belonged to the doctor whose surgery was in Greville Road, opposite the pub.

Records show that members of the Clark family were landlords of the Hen and Chicken in the late 1700s, including Elizabeth and Jacob Clark who also owned a timber yard on Coronation Road, the name continuing in the Bristol timber trade today. Their son, Samuel, a person of some standing in the area, petitioned for the building of St Paul's church, Coronation Road. The family continued to run the pub until at least 1950, when Martin Clark was publican. Kevin Summerill recalls the pub in more recent times: 'My parents used to have their own tankards [there]. The landlords were Mr and Mrs Lawrence. There was a big fire in the 1960s and our tankards went up with it. It was almost like a religion to go in on a Sunday lunchtime while your mum was cooking the lunch. At that age, if you did go out for a drink you'd go down town. You perhaps didn't want go down Bedminster – it always had a bit of reputation. Besides, you might be spotted by a family member if you decided to have a sneaky drink in a local pub.'

# 208-206 GEORGE HATHWAY, BOOTMAKER

(NOW CO-OPERATIVE, SUPERMARKET)

George Hathway in the doorway of his boot shop. The site is now occupied by a supermarket. The Kensitas cigarette poster offering prizes of an 'Austin a day' dates it to c1932. On the left is the Hen and Chicken, with a customer leaving the off-licence. On the right of the shop (whose fabric is looking quite ancient) is almost certainly the original Georgian bay-fronted Hen and Chicken portrayed in the Parkman sketch. The fascia reads A Chilcott, a grocer trading from number 206.

👉 **Diana Brown, who was brought up above the fish and chip shop opposite, remembers that this 'bomb site was left derelict after the war.'** Kevin and Lin Cox remember the spot following redevelopment in the 1960s: 'It used to be Welch's car showroom with a glass front, a big place. I'm sure there was a small library around the back where you could borrow books.' Eventually a Fine Fare supermarket opened here in 1973, housed in a functional single storey building. Since then its occupants have included budget supermarket Whoppas, Helibeds, and the current Co-op.

For many years before the war, a shop on this site (208) was occupied by George Hathway, bootmaker. George was born in 1865 and he and his wife, Ellen had nine children. Ernest, born around 1900, was the youngest and together with his wife Maud ran the vegetable shop (85) on the opposite side of the street.

# 204 HAWKINS & SONS, FURNITURE REMOVERS

(NOW HAART, ESTATE AGENTS)

👉 **Built at the start of the twentieth century, number**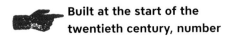

**204, the first in this row of shops, was at some point later divided into two narrower properties.** Diana Brown recalls how, in the 1960s, 'Mrs Appleton ran a sweet shop and tobacconists. She had a little library, and next door was Hawkins removals.' Alan Hawkins remembers his father's business well:

*My father, Reg, and his brother Horace went into the family business started by their father Charles. It started as an egg round and gradually went over to furniture removals. In the early years the business, built up in south Bristol, grew. [The then new estates of] Knowle West and Bedminster Down put C Hawkins and Sons on the map. I joined the firm the day after I left school at the age of 15. All the years I worked, I was treated exactly the same as all the other employees – same wages, same conditions. Soon after I started my Grandad died and the two brothers took control. They were a good team and both knew the trade inside out. The firm grew over the years and we were running ten vehicles by 1970. Our vehicles were all built locally. We would purchase a coach chassis and it would be taken to the workshop at the corner of Cannon Street and Dean Lane to be built and then painted in the building next to the Star. [It was] a great pride to take delivery of a new shining van made by top quality people here in South Bristol. Hawkins and Sons had grown so much that we were ripe for a takeover which happened in 1970 and finally sold out to a larger company, Bullen Transport.*

Tuesday and every Saturday. They catch the bus up from the flats, have their bit of food and coffee and walk back down and do their shopping. It gets them out of the house for a while.'

June, one of the regulars, had been coming to the Tasty Stop almost every day since she moved nearby 13 years before: 'When you lives on your own, it's a bit of company, isn't it?' June used to arrive before 10am and buy a cup of tea, then chat with the other regulars: 'Sometimes I have another cup of tea. They are very good, they don't mind you sitting here.' The regulars used to have their own seats and June said that they knew each other by their first names and send birthday cards to each other. Tasty Stop was busy on days when City played at home. Trade varied on other days, as Ann recalled: 'It's hard to predict what the ordinary day will bring. Sometimes I'll be rushed off my feet; other times it is quite quiet.' Sadly, this North Street institution closed in October 2014.

The firm of C Hawkins & Sons was started in 1918. A warehouse was built so that customers' furniture could be stored while it was in transit, and this is probably the location of this image. During the Second World War, some of the vans were apparently requisitioned by the War Office and never seen again. The firm was based at 145 North Street from 1930-37, and then at 204 North Street

## 202 TASTY STOP

(NOW EMPTY AND UNDERGOING RENOVATION)

👉 **Customers would always get a warm welcome from Ann behind the counter at the Tasty Stop café.** Ann had been in the catering trade for a long time, starting work in the canteen at a local factory. Ann describes her job at Tasty Stop: 'You get students coming in at the weekend – the all-day breakfast is popular with them – but the weekdays are when most of our regulars come.' A good number of people used the cafe for many years, one group of friends going there at least three days every week and frequently staying for a couple of hours, as Ann recalled: 'One comes for his breakfast at about 9am, then his friends join him for coffee. Three older ladies come in every

June, one of the Tasty Stop's regulars, 2013

**101**

One of Vicky's customers proposed 'knitting the iconic buildings of Bristol,' which became "Briswool." The 3-D model of the city was created by around 100 people. Vicky said that her shop had been 'a woolly world filled with crochet trees, knitted houses, the SS Great Britain and Cabot Tower perched on top of the woolly undergrowth.' In the team were a seven-year-old girl who made penguins for the zoo, as well as knitters in their late 70s. Briswool went on display for the 2014 South Bristol Arts Trail, attracting around 4,000 visitors to Paper Village

# 200 PAPER VILLAGE

**Diana Brown remembers this shop when she was a child as Foster Electrical Supplies, 'a lighting company – they sold everything for wholesale.'** Vicky Harrison opened Paper Village in 2010. She has lived in the area for over twenty years and remembers the time when 'North Street was quite a different place, a lot of good shops. [Then] it went downhill and a lot of the shops closed. I started thinking that there was very little on this part of North Street and what a shame that was, so I decided to do something about it.'

Paper Village is partly a conventional shop, an Aladdin's cave of craft materials and equipment, but Vicky sees her business as much more than this: 'It is a shop, a project and a community group.' She runs various events here, such as 'Paper Illuminated' which produces paper lanterns for Christmas street parades in the centre of Bedminster. The shop acts as the creative hub for an almost endless list of community art projects, such as 'Crochet and Knitting Jam', creating an origami garden, and a competition for the best decorated garden gate, run in conjunction with 'Playing Out', an organisation based in a nearby shop with the aim of encouraging children's play through temporary street closures. In 2014, Vicky masterminded 'Briswool', a huge 3D model of Bristol, created in knitting, crochet, needle felt and bead-weaving.

As well as running courses and workshops, Vicky's vision includes resourcing and supporting individual creativity in lots of other ways. She designs and cuts stencil patterns on request and has a communal sewing machine in the shop. Paper Village also provides a loan service, providing rubber stamps, cup cake decorating kits, stencils, books and a wealth of other materials. Another important aim of Paper Village is to encourage people to share resources. For example, they bring in their old knitting magazines, which, as Vicky says, 'they share, swap or just give away. I'm probably the only shop that gets given heaps of stuff – from people bringing me cakes they've made me, to bringing their old pattern books.'

Vicky doesn't regard internet shopping as a threat to high street commerce, but more of a social problem: 'If everyone starts shopping on the internet, nobody will meet anybody. That may not seem that abhorrent to twenty year olds, but there will come a time when they realise how lonely and isolated people can be.' Vicky is also concerned that some of the recent changes to North Street which she knows some people refer to as a 'new, vibrant feel', have not always

Vicky Harrison with one of her simpler tools, 2013

benefited older residents in the local community. 'A lot of older people are really isolated around here. A lot of my customers remember going to the [now demolished] Luckwell Club for their "eighteenth", for weddings, and when the Bingo closed that changed the area tremendously too.'

Vicky sums up Paper Village as 'a social meeting point. Some people were quite isolated, then Paper Village came along and over time they've got to know other people because of coming to things here.'

# 198 FREEMAN, HARDY & WILLIS
(NOW UPFEST)

From the 1920s, number 198 housed a bootmakers which traded for at least 40 years as a branch of the national chain, **Freeman, Hardy & Willis.** Diana Brown went to work there when she was 15: 'We had a part-time lady, Mrs Fowler, who came in at 1pm so we could go to dinner. We'd shut half day on Wednesdays.' According to Diana, the shop sold 'men's, women's and children's shoes, wellingtons and handbags. We had a measuring board for children. We took in repairs which we sent away.' As well as working in sales, Diana did other things in the shop:

*I would polish the wooden floors and Hoover the carpets. There was a lovely wooden fireplace, floor to ceiling, with a big mirror and shelves that all had to be cleaned. In the shop was a big cupboard which held shoe polish, laces, stockings, gloves and handbags.*

Diana earned commission on goods she sold: 'The customer had one receipt and one went in the drawer. The manager, Mr Monks, knew what had been sold and checked the money which went into the safe.' There were regular deliveries and new styles, although 'it was no fun carrying cartons of men's heavy working boots. Most weeks it could be twenty cartons, and then they had to be put away in order.' When there was a quiet moment she would have to 'dust all the boxes, and as the shelves were floor to ceiling it was a lot of boxes.' Despite the hard work Diana says '[I] did enjoy my work.' The manager had a ginger cat called Fred. He was popular with the customers and would sit on their laps. Children would love to follow him round, and when it was sunny Fred would get into the shop window and go to sleep.

Diana remembers the customers and how busy it could get:

*Men were easy customers, women were fussy and children were lovely.*

*Fridays were manic because Wills' [workers] got paid and they'd come in and spend their money. If they couldn't afford the shoes my boss would keep them under the cupboard and they'd pay every week until it was paid off. We had to remember all the names of the shoes. Mr Monks wouldn't let a customer go out without buying something. You'd sometimes get customers trying on eight pairs of shoes and they more often than not would go back to the first! When we had the floods in 1966, I was on my own and I sold out of wellingtons. They were about £1 a pair. We used to have a lady come in called Gert. She'd plonk herself down and have a cigarette, we'd give her a cup of tea and she'd stay and have her cigarette and then go off. She always carried a bag but we never found*

Mr Monks, the manager of Freeman, Hardy & Willis, who lived over the shop (198) c1960s. Diana Brown recalls a large garden at the back. Fifty years later, Steve Hayles of UPFEST moved in to find it was 'like a mini-orchard, full of fruit trees and bushes.' UPFEST has kept some of this haven, and also made the back into a painting spot with an artist's studio

Artist at work at North Street Green, UPFEST, May 2013

Crowds during UPFEST, outside the festival's headquarters (198), May 2013

out what was in it.

Jack House remembers the shop before the Second World War:

*I have a memory, I couldn't have been more than four, of there being a fire at Freeman Hardy & Willis. I must have been in Agate Street and there was this wonderful sight of the fire engine with all the firemen stood on the outside of the engine, going across the tram lines then leaping off and rushing in!*

When Freeman Hardy Willis closed (the '&' had been dropped by then), the shop became a Barnardo's charity shop and Diana's mother worked there as a volunteer.

## 198 UPFEST

**To all appearances, this shop is just a small art gallery, but is in fact headquarters of UPFEST which organizes the largest urban paint festival in Europe.** Steve Hayles, UPFEST's founder, explains that 'street art' is not just about graffiti: 'It's not a style but simply describes where the art is located. For example, we have illustrators and fine artists who create work during the festival. People say Banksy is a street artist, but foremost he is a stencil artist.'

In 2006, having worked for an insurance company for about ten years and being passionate about art, Steve tried volunteering in the live arts scene in Bristol. 'It was all a bit cliquey,' he recalls, but after he was made redundant he decided to take the plunge with a risky idea that turned into UPFEST:

*We sent a cheeky email to the*

Tobacco Factory and said we've got all these artists and want to do a live art event. I then told a number of artists I'd got to know that I had this great venue – neither of which had been confirmed – so it was kind of a double bluff. But the Tobacco Factory said 'Yes' and the first festival took place in their car park in October 2008.

The first festival attracted about 750 visitors and 50 artists. The next year the festival lasted two days and has grown year by year since then, so that by 2013 it had 25,000 visitors with both temporary and permanent art works created by 300 artists along the length of North Street. Steve describes how UPFEST operates:

*The festival is non profit-making, we get just enough funding to run it. There's no visitor or artist fee. A number of businesses sponsor the festival and a lot of the work is done by volunteers. For example, locals might come in and volunteer to spend hours painting boards white. I remember one Friday afternoon a local builder brought his mates and they all helped put up the boards.*

The festival is marshalled by volunteers from the National Association for Children of Alcoholics (NACOA) and Steve is justly proud that UPFEST has raised about £30,000 for charity. Because of the mix of people attracted to the festival, young as well as old, the charity's profile has been raised too.

Steve doesn't shy away from the controversial nature of permanent street art in North Street. How does he respond to the criticism from some local people who complain that the permanent work on walls and shop shutters makes the whole area scruffy? 'We don't want to alienate people. For example, one year some local people were saying they wanted less graffiti, so the following year we had mostly "photo realistic" art.' He knows it won't be right for everyone every time. If there has been anything offensive it's been removed:

*I think there have been two pieces and I've removed them. I know not everyone agrees with street art, but some of them can see that there's a trade off. One shopkeeper came up to me and said 'I've managed to pay more bills this month – I sold out of masking tape, white paint!'*

The shop serves several purposes:

*We sell spray paint; we do framing; use it as a bit of a HQ [as] we do other urban art stuff around the country. We also sell affordable art work and have exhibitions every six weeks or so and we rent out art we've got. We couldn't survive as just a gallery, or paint shop – or just the festival.*

The business has also developed Steve's sense of community and approach to the area in which he lives and works. He is now a board member for the Bedminster Town Plan. Initially his interest was just in running UPFEST, but now, 'working with the arts and culture for regeneration is definitely something we've moved into. For example we worked on the Bugs trail [individually painted giant bugs fixed above shop fronts] that is about getting art into our high streets.'

What of the future of UPFEST? 'As the area is becoming more popular, many of our derelict sites are being developed,' says Steve. That's partly why for the 2015 Festival, Steve has ideas that could stretch the display to cover nearly two miles of south Bristol. 'We're still here doing what we love and have managed to establish the largest urban art festival in Europe!'

# 196 BOBBIE BURNS
(NOW SOUTH WEST UPHOLSTERY)

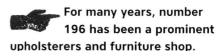 **For many years, number 196 has been a prominent upholsterers and furniture shop.** Prior to being taken over by South West Upholstery in 2013, it traded under the name of the original owner 'Bobbie Burns' and run latterly by Paul Harris:

*My father's name was Victor Matthew Harris and he bought the business off Bobbie Burns in the early 1960s. Bobbie Burns himself was a very big lad. He must have been about 25 stone. He was a whisky drinker and used to go in the*

Paul Harris in his upholstery workshop at Bobbie Burns (196), 2013

Victor Harris in Bobbie Burns c1960. The 'Spring Furnishing Event' is on, and customers are urged 'Don't look, Buy Now.' The pane of decorated glass was from the original pre-war St Francis's Church in North Street

*Hen and Chicken. He used to do a lot of work for the Ministry of Defence, making curtains, supplying carpets and a lot of their chairs. He did all the pubs around and outside Bristol and used to sell furniture as well from this shop, which*

Bobbie Burns (196), 1993. The building to the right has now been replaced with a modern shop. Prior to this the space was used as storage for John Waite's building business.

*was the showroom.*

*I began working for my Dad when I was about 16. We used to make furniture, solid wood frame beech frames and have the spring frames made, then we used to cover them and sell them to Haskins [a Shepton Mallet family firm]. We also sold beds, headboards, three piece suites, curtains and carpets but as it got more modern we didn't do so well, so we started doing upholstery.*

*There used to be about ten of us here plus myself and my Dad and we had a rep on the road. We had some big contracts – Hall's Brewery making bench seats with button backs for their pubs; office furniture for Barclay's Bank and NatWest. We also did a lot of polishing – French polished all the furniture in*

*the Rocks Hotel near the Suspension Bridge. We used to do about 1,000 office chairs a week. We could start at five in the morning until ten at night. It got too much, so we stopped doing the office chairs and kept on the domestic furniture. I just picked up the trade from my Dad, I didn't have an apprenticeship. We put things which have been half-done in the window so people can see what work goes into it. I get trade from all over the place. Nowadays there's four of us working full time. My mother, Evelyn May Harris, is 89 and she still works here six days a week. [Mrs Harris died in 2013].*

South West Upholstery, a thriving company, owned and managed by father and son Andy and Ryan Ball, took over the shop in 2013. Established in a business park, the firm relocated to 196 North Street 'to catch the passing trade,' says Andy. To preserve the past history of the shop, South West Upholstery sells reupholstered vintage furniture branded as 'The Bobbie Burns Collection' which it describes as 'classic mid-century design to unusual one-off pieces upholstered in bespoke fabrics and leathers. We are extremely proud to be keeping the history of 'Bobbie Burns' alive within Bristol.'

# 192 – 178

**Number 192, currently Watkins' solicitors, is a listed building dating from around 1780 and set back from the street.** In more recent times Diana Brown recalls how 'John Waite and his family lived in the house.' They had a timber yard,

Number 192, one of North Street's four listed buildings, Winter 2012

Number 186 extends to the pavement from the Georgian house behind. Over the past century it has housed many trades, including a milliner, motor engineer, coal merchants and furnishers

selling timber and plasterboard, run by Mr Waite and his son-in-law.

Next along the road is a terrace of late eighteenth century houses (190 to 186), also set back; then a row of Victorian houses which meets the corner of Upper Sydney Street. The names of the buildings here have changed over time; Carlton Place, Carlton House, The Villa and Carlton Terrace. Some may either be the same buildings or replacements. However, Carlton Place is where Joseph Cottle, publisher of works by the celebrated British poets, Robert Southey and William Wordsworth, lived.

Of the original rank of five Georgian houses, three remain, each having a single storey extension from the original house to the street front. Local people recall a wallpaper shop, Brunel Eager, and a pram shop operating from these premises. The tragic story of the 'Bedminster Hermits', reported in The

*Bristol Mercury* in 1888, describes a little of the history of these properties. Apparently a Mr Thomas Hort bought the grazing land, farm and nurseries hereabouts and built the five houses in the 1830s, choosing the best for himself, 'The Villa'. Eventually his family inherited these and The Villa was lived in by his three unmarried daughters. The newspaper report, written in true Victorian 'Gothic' style, tells of how in spite of their inheritance, the sisters lived in extreme poverty and had become "so eccentric that every window was smashed in. They protected the windows with trellis work and rags." Inside, the ground floor was derelict, with just one chair which had three legs, "a pile of bricks did duty for the fourth." Upstairs, most of the furniture had been burnt and there was "a rubbish heap of fine crockery broken into minute pieces." Holes in the roof were used

to collect rain water. The sorry state of the final remaining sister, Matilda Hort, was reported because she was discovered following a fire, "the head being completely burnt off." The inquest learned that some local people were in the habit of provoking her, and "in place of flower beds were rough heaps of stones which had been thrown at the windows."

The corner shop (178) was a fish shop, Cook and Sons, from the 1950s for over 30 years. Roy Gallop recalls that: *It was run by a guy and someone we thought was his missus. They used to have this banter going on. You used to go in there just for the conversation – it was brilliant! He was a funny little guy with a moustache and a cap, a bit like Andy Capp.*

Like many similar corner shops, it has been converted into a house.

**CHAPTER 23**

# UPPER SYDNEY STREET TO MYRTLE STREET 176-156

Number 156. Jeff Johnston, who worked in North Street, recalls that at Jordan's 'you used to get the best doughnuts in the world.' Undated

**B**edminster's biggest 'Do It Yourself' (DIY) shop traded here for around forty years, supplying everything from good quality tools to wallpaper, cement and doormats. Nails could be bought by the pound, or 'three or four screws at a time', recalls Frank Phillips; various paint colours mixed, and timber cut to size by knowledgeable members of the Cashman family and their staff. The business started off here in the early 1960s as Cashman & Sons, roofing contractors, then extending to become Cashman's Do-It-Yourself Arcades. Tony Cashman's successful business grew in the heyday of DIY and expanded to take over adjacent shops, including hairdresser Diplaros at the corner (176). This section of the shop was devoted to selling cane furniture.

Robert Cashman worked in the shop on Saturdays, Sundays and bank holidays, from about the age of 13 until it closed down: 'There were about eight staff employed by my father. The business had at one time seven or eight shops stretched over the South West, with about 150 employees, run from offices in Old Market. The Bedminster shop, I understand, was the first.'

The Cashman's shop eventually became known as Cash Save Mica, but its days were numbered in the face of competition from nearby DIY superstores. The cane furniture business remained for a while, but eventually closed completely. By 2009 the building had been demolished and a Tesco 'Metro' supermarket erected in its place.

The terrace between Upper Sydney Street and Myrtle Street was built in the 1890s. Most of the row has always been residential with just the two corner buildings being shops. Over the century these shops were occupied by butchers, Cashman's, grocers, fruit shops and the like. For about 30 years, from the late 1930s, the local removal firm of Percy Bawn operated from here. Number 156 at the end of this row, on the corner of Myrtle Street, traded as a bakers for nearly 100 years. It was run by George Bennett, then Ernest Jordan took over soon after the First World War. Mr Tucker who lived nearby has fond memories of the bakers from the late 1930s:

*When my mother and her sister Ciss went shopping, they would dump my cousin Michael and myself upon Grandpa. At lunchtime, he would march across the road to Jordan's Bakery and purchase a large loaf. This he would cut in two lengthwise, the pieces were then spread with about a quarter pound of butter. He then gave us a whole half each. On other occasions a helping of chips were stuffed into a large hollowed out loaf, again cut lengthwise. We would then swill this down with lemonade.*

Barrie Wheeler also remembers the temptation of this shop while he walked from the bus stop to South Street School: 'I would buy a penny loaf a couple of mornings a week – the bread was still hot. On cold mornings this was as good as having a bowl of porridge.'

# MYRTLE STREET TO EXMOOR STREET 154-142

**A**t one time this was a row of seven shops, built in the opening years of the twentieth century, all trading in everyday commodities such as groceries, meat, drapery and newspapers. By the 1970s, the last remaining shop was Bristol Flooring. A few local residents recall the former shops, which include the sophisticated-sounding Maison Francis, later known as Francis Coiffeur, and a grocers shop, one in the Butt family's chain.

## 146 MAISON FRANCIS
(NOW RESIDENTIAL)

 **An earlier hairdressing business was taken over after the Second World War to become Maison Francis, ladies' hairdresser, the allure of 'Parisian style' having reached south Bristol.** Valerie Pearce started work in the shop in 1959 and remembers its proprietor well:

*Francis had a little moustache, he used to wear a beret and drive a Citroen car – but he wasn't French. I started there as a Friday night/Saturday girl doing odd jobs, sweeping the floor, shampooing hair, putting ladies under the driers and taking them out. There*

The staff at Maison Francis (146) c1960. Front row, L to R: Audrey; Sylvia; Jillian; Brenda; Verlie; Angela. Back row, L to R: Dinah; Frank Manning, proprietor; centre, Jane Manning, his daughter; Vivienne; Lesley

*were several of us there. From there I got an apprenticeship with him for three years and then I stayed working there until 1965. From the outside it wasn't very big but it went back a long way. There were three floors and all were used, with twenty-six people working there. I was known as Angela, my second name, decided by the boss because there was already a Valerie there and she was senior to me. Customers called us by our first name but Mrs Locke was always called Mrs Locke. The proprietor, Frank [Francis] was known as Mr Manning. There was a chap used to walk past the salon every*

Marilyn (L) and Angela outside Maison Francis (146). Undated

109

Audrey (L) and Vivienne, known as 'Bubbles', at Maison Francis (146), 1964

*dinner time flexing his muscles and all the girls used to go mad! He was the man who [later] did the Green Cross Code advert [Dave Prowse, a Bristolian weightlifting champion who played the role of Darth Vader in Star Wars]. Friday night was 'Wills' night' in North Street! Come four o'clock you'd be looking at the clock and have everything ready at the basin – the towels and the gowns – because once the Wills' girls came in you'd be busy. They'd run up the road (all the appointments were the same time) to try and be the first ones in to get their hair washed, partly dried and then put into rollers. We had about four or five basins and it was like a conveyor belt for about an hour. On a Friday we'd finish at 7.30pm although it would sometimes be eight o'clock when I'd come out.*

# 144 BUTT'S STORES

(NOW BRISTOL FLOORING, CARPETS AND VINYLS)

**David Butt is the great-grandson of Walter Henry Butt who ran a prosperous grocery firm with at least five shops in south Bristol, including two in North Street.** Walter's son John married Dorothy Knowles in 1920, thereby joining two families of local grocers. David's knowledge of both the Butts and the Knowles families not only illustrates the rise and fall of the grocery trade over fifty years, but highlights how personalities shaped the two family businesses in very different ways.

Walter Butt, born 1865, started an apprenticeship in a grocers shop in Cardiff. He moved to Bristol and bought his first shop, 7 North Street, in 1892. He always used this as his main shop, the rear of the premises serving as the company office. 'He was an entrepreneur, and always wanted to expand the business. Maybe this is why he called the business Butt's Stores, not Butt & Sons,' says David. By 1903 the shop had expanded into number 144.

For the first twenty years, Walter appears to have prospered. From living over the shop in North Street, he moved to Stackpool Road nearby, but eventually left the area in the early 1920s and bought a large house in Brislington. He owned some of his stores and leased others and at its height, the Butt's Stores business was running nine shops. Later, both of his sons, Edward and John, worked for Walter.

The business depended on customers having a rapport and relationship with the shop staff and proprietor. Walter Butt regularly advertised in *The Bristol Mercury* for staff: 'Experienced, smart gentleman to work in Butt's Stores.' Walter apparently preferred male shop assistants in the belief that the 'bread winners' had more incentive to perform and keep their jobs than a married woman relying on their husband's income. He continued running and owning the business until he died in August 1938 when it was widely believed that he was a millionaire. The two sons inherited the business, although with stringent conditions in their father's Will about leaving the business and properties in trust.

David Butt's uncle, Vernon, and his cousin, Brian Butt, both remember the shops. Brian recalls going into his father's shop in North Street, with its 'blocks of cheese from Canada cut with a wire, loose sugar in the drawer, and weighing up loose tea from a chest.' A trap door led to the cellar where the goods were kept. The shops operated half-day closing on Wednesday afternoons, but used to stay open as late as 11pm when people would come out from the pub and do their shopping.

As children, David's father Lionel and his uncle Vernon used to go to the Butt's wholesale store at 2a Merrywood Road to play. Vernon remembers 'splitting a bag, but the manager didn't say a thing. Walter Henry used to come out and say to his grandchildren: "I've got an urgent message. Would you mind taking it to Mr So-and-So" at one of the stores, giving us an envelope with a note inside. We would run to the shop, whereupon the manager would open the envelope to find a note saying "Would you please give the boys two biscuits."'

At the end of the nineteenth century, George Frederick Knowles was also setting up as a grocer, by 1910 not only owning a shop at 201 Hotwell Road, but also one at 236 North Street. It was the marriage of George's daughter Dorothy Knowles to Walter Butt's son that joined the two families of grocers together in 1920, although the businesses remained separate. It is their differences, as recalled by David Butt, that help us understand more about approaches to trade:

*Walter's businesses employed well over 50 people. Undoubtedly Walter was an entrepreneur, and he was said to be keen to be known and be seen as successful, whereas Frederick Knowles seemed happy with his three shops. A family story about Walter's desire to be noticed is that he was always the last to enter St Luke's Church [Brislington] on a Sunday morning, leaving his house just as the final bell was tolling, so that the congregation would turn round*

*and notice him! He was described as 'hard-nosed' and striving to increase his social standing.*

In contrast, George Knowles was described as being 'happy with his own lot.' It was common for him to allow people to have items 'on tick', and George's generosity was apparent when, every Christmas, he would go through his books and write off the debts of some of his poorer customers. George Knowles is reported to have had a different approach to being a supplier of food to deprived neighbourhoods. The two entrepreneurs prospered in the years after the First World War: Walter moved to a bigger property and George to the desirable area of Clifton Wood, although he later moved back near North Street to support his daughter.

In January 1941, Butt's wholesale premises were destroyed in an air raid and after the war both the Knowles' and the Butt's businesses slowly declined. Members of the Butt family say that Walter blamed the Co-operative store for his demise. The business finally went bankrupt. The Knowles company ended in 1956, victim not only of post-war slum clearance and road-widening scheme in Hotwells

which affected shops there, but also because the firm had depended heavily on supplying the Campbell 'White Funnel' paddle steamers which operated on the River Avon from Hotwells, but we were forced to stop during the war.

After Butt's closed, number 144 continued in use as a grocers, Hind's. However, the premises was later linked with the notorious 'Brink's-MAT' robbery which took place at Heathrow Airport on 26th November 1983 when six armed robbers, posing as security guards, broke into the high security warehouse at Heathrow stealing total of £26 million, at the time the biggest haul in British criminal history. Eventually a number of people were convicted, while others, including a director of the North Street scrap jewellery and gold business, Scadlynn's, run from above the furniture shop at 144, were acquitted. The nearby Barclay's Bank had become suspicious of the large payments from the business registered at 144 and arrests ensued.

Walter Butt was a member of the local Federation of Grocers, which was part of a national association. When the annual conference was held in Bristol Walter and the organisers rose to the occasion, and delegates were wined and dined with the sponsorship of local and national food producers, keen to promote their products. On the inside of this 1926 conference programme is a studio portrait of Walter Butt in his chain of office, 'President-designate of the Federation of Grocers' Associations of the United Kingdom.'

# EXMOOR STREET TO DARTMOOR STREET, THEN TO KING WILLIAM STREET 140-112

**CHAPTER 25**

**I**n the 1880s, this section of North Street, in contrast to the rapidly developing surrounding areas, still had a rural appearance. North House with its extensive grounds, stood here. The building of the suburb of Southville at the end of the nineteenth century coincided with the construction of fourteen shops – originally selling sweets, fried fish, pork and millinery – at this point on North Street. Nowadays, shoppers in search of food stuffs along this stretch of the road will have empty baskets. All but one of the shops which once stood here were destroyed in the infamous 'Good Friday raid' on April 11th 1941, the same raid also destroying property on much of the other side of the road.

During the following sixty years, the derelict land was used for the sale of cars and caravans. One or two shops came and went in what remained of the buildings, the only surviving pre-war shop being that of George Dyer, baker. By 2006, rising land prices tipped the balance, the used car lots gradually disappeared and both sites were redeveloped for housing. The only remaining trader along this stretch is Petrie Glazing (112), the owner, Bob Petrie and his colleagues providing a friendly service, from cutting small panes of glass to fabricating large double-glazed window units.

# KING WILLIAM STREET TO FAIRFIELD ROAD 110-82

**CHAPTER 26**

**M**aps of this section show that by the 1850s some of the land bordering what was still a country lane had already been developed with terraced housing, while a few fields and orchards still remained. With the fields yet to be encroached on by the future Southville, no side roads led from North Street as they do today. However by the 1870s King William Street had been built, with the Masonic Hotel on its corner with North Street. The terrace to the east of the Masonic Hotel was largely residential, although by 1910 several properties had been converted to shops, among which were a hatters, a hairdressers and a dealer in cycles and phonographs.

Like the area round Exmoor and Dartmoor Streets, this part of North Street was badly damaged by bombing in the same raid that destroyed the properties where Gaywood House on the other side of North Street was later built. Five or so of the houses alongside the Masonic Hotel (**see 110**) suffered direct hits, the Hotel surviving with minor damage. The large, undeveloped piece of land here has been used for the sale of second-hand cars ever since, trading for several decades as Sparkes Garage, more recently as Anthony's Motors. Jeff Johnston remembers buying his first car, 'a Ford Popular there, for about £117, when I first got my driving licence in 1965.'

A lane in the centre of the original terrace led to industrial buildings

The bomb-site (92) which served as a used car lot for many years after the War, later became a petrol station. Supporting this picket against Shell in 1986 is Dawn Primarolo (in white dress), who became the local Member of Parliament the following year

Wartime damage exposed to view the Cooperative factory (100), with its tall chimney. Most recently trading as Clifton Paints, the site was cleared for housing in 2014

which, in the early 1920s, housed the Cooperative Laundry. By the beginning of the Second World War it had become the Bristol Cooperative Society Small Goods Factory, remembered by Sheila Williams: 'In the 1950s, when I was at Southville School we used to have our cookery lesson at South Street School. At the end of the day we used to walk along an alley alongside the building. It was a cheese factory and it used to stink like mad!'

From the Masonic, on past Anthony's Cars, the remaining three shops (90-86) offer a mix of the practical, the exotic and the derelict. Local people recall how corn dealer, George Wishart moved to the first shop in the row, now the Co-operative Pharmacy, after having been bombed out just a few doors up the road (118). Muriel and Ken Eley remember the shop well: 'Ken's dad used to get all his chickens there. They used to have a cardboard cut-out picture in the window, of a hen and an elephant having a tug of war, with the caption 'Our chicks are as strong as an elephant!' – the same slogan used by Sidney Collins at number 254. By the 1960s it had become The Bandbox, ladies outfitters, as Valerie Pearce recalls: 'My mother used to buy her clothes there. I used to do the owner's hair but she was so fussy. She would always take the comb from me when I'd finished and "tweek" her hair herself. She sold nice clothes and had a range of prices. She'd change her stock all the time.'

The last of the three shops (86) was for many years the Auroma Stores, now standing empty. Jeff Johnston remembers it as a 'junk shop', and Dave Russell recalls its more elegant days in the 1960s and early 70s, as Smith's, Gents tailors: 'Every Christmas, I would have a free shirt and probably a tie as well. Lots of different places would give you something at Christmas.' Dave's job as a driver's assistant meant that he travelled along North Street on a regular basis. The middle shop in the parade is Tattootime (**see 88**) with Stafford's Launderette (**see 82**) on the corner.

**113**

The Masonic lit for Christmas (110), 2012

UPFEST 'Snarl' on the Masonic, 2013

Jantzen Derrick topples a pile of pennies collected for charity in the Masonic. Looking on is Lilly Whiting, who married the landlord Len Whiting (L) after the death of her first husband Bill. Bill Derrick was Jantzen's great-uncle. Jantzen, who still lives locally, dates the photo to c1960, not long after he had started his professional footballing career with Bristol City

# 110 THE MASONIC

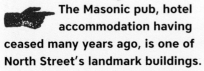 **The Masonic pub, hotel accommodation having ceased many years ago, is one of North Street's landmark buildings.** The current landlord, Martin Bidder, has managed the pub for over sixteen years and has always worked in the pub trade: 'Forty-four years. I started down The Star [4-6 North Street], then The House that Jack Built on St John's Lane, then down Weston [super Mare] for a few years; then I was down the Whitening Yard [The Ship and Castle.]'

The Masonic is a 'free house', owned by a small company which employs Martin as landlord. He is helped by five part-time staff. From the outside, the pub looks quite small, but once inside the bar area is spacious. When he took over the pub, Martin knocked down a few walls and built the skittle alley.

*When it comes to business, we do alright. The customers are all local – Bedminster mostly and Bedminster Down. Then you've got Knowle and Hartcliffe. We've got the skittle alley and darts so people come down for matches. We're open five nights and Sunday lunchtime. I shut at three o'clock on Sunday – that's the only day I shut. We don't get any trouble and if anyone misbehaves, they're out!*

Martin is convinced that the area has changed. 'At one time the landlords all knew one another and used to meet and go drinking together. Now you keep yourself to yourself really.' Martin plans to leave the pub trade in the near future. 'I've enjoyed the pub life, but I want a bit of time to meself. I'll miss a few people.'

The Masonic has many loyal customers. As one put it: 'It's a great pub, great landlord and staff. He serves a good pint, that's all that matters.' 'You'll always feel welcome and find someone to talk to in here.'

# 88 TATTOOTIME

 **Dean Reed opened his first tattoo parlour at 173 North Street in 1993.** After three years, Tattootime was so successful that he expanded and moved to number 88. Dean has 'been involved in tattooing' since he was 14. While watching and learning from friends tattooing at home, he knew that tattooing was something he wanted to do. He was never short of anyone to practise on, so what had been a hobby became a successful business.

Inside the waiting room, prospective clients view a gallery of work that Dean and his experienced colleagues can create. Many people, however, know what they want before they arrive. As Dean says, 'Ninety percent of people come in already armed with their own stuff from the internet.' Dean and his team are heavily tattooed – walking adverts for the quality of their work – and will tackle most pieces, large or small. Dean works hard to dispel the idea that tattooing is mostly just for 'tough guys.' He agrees it is not for everyone, but, as he says, 'it's not going to change you as a person having a tattoo done. You have one done and then you wake up the next day and you realise you are actually the same person.' Tattootime's customers show how far the traditional image has shifted. 'A lot of our clients are ladies,' he says. 'We don't want to be associated with one type of people [and] welcome to all age groups. The oldest lady I've tattooed was sixty-eight for her first tattoo – and then she came back on her 72nd birthday for her second while her friends waited for her

outside in the car.' Equally, Dean knows when to say no. He's not a great fan of tattooing hands, faces and necks, especially on younger clients. 'I believe you should think ahead and consider what you might be happy with now, in ten years' time you might not be thinking the same way.' He usually sends these young enthusiasts away, 'rather than just taking their money.'

When asked what he thought were the reasons for his success, Dean said: 'I think we've got a good reputation. People are pleased to come here.' He also follows trends: 'Piercing was a fashionable thing, although it seems to have faded away a bit now.' In the early days of the business, when tattoo parlours were less commonplace, he advertised on television which brought in clients from as far afield as Gloucestershire and Swindon. He even has clients who come in from abroad. But now, although there is more competition, it is 'word of mouth' that brings his clients here. As for the future of North Street, Dean is worried about 'rumblings of permit car-parking, but North Street is where our home is. It's up to us to keep our game together and I'm always looking for new ideas.'

# 82 STAFFORD'S LAUNDERETTE

 **The final building in this row, on the corner with Fairfield Road, is a branch of Staffords Launderette, a Bristol firm.** The premises were rebuilt after wartime bombing and it has been a launderette

One of Dean's window displays at Tattootime (88), 2013

Dean Reed of Tattootime (88) with a tattoo machine, 2013. A small piece of work may only take twenty minutes, but for larger pieces Dean doesn't work for more than a couple of hours at a time, as it is demanding work for both the artist and the customer

Sarah Buckland performs in Show of Strength Theatre Company's Trading Local, at Staffords Launderette, February 2009

DRY CLEANING RECEPTION

Pet Wrigglesworth welcomes customers to Staffords Launderette (82), 2013

for over fifty years. Pet Wrigglesworth is in charge and she believes that it is the second oldest launderette still open in Bristol.

Pet is the friendly face of washing and dry cleaning in North Street. She makes sure her customers can work the washing machines and tumble-driers, takes in dry cleaning to be sent away, does the 'service washes' and keeps everything spick and span. And she knows what's going on in the street. She's been approached at least once by the Police, asking if she had spotted a particular suspect through the large shop windows. Pet's customers are of all ages and types. She says, 'People think it's a student zone, but it's not anymore.' Certainly some of her visitors are just occasional – people who come in and say, 'I haven't been in a launderette since I was a student; [the ones] who come in with a suitcase of washing after

they've been on holiday. If it is going to take you forty minutes to do it here and a week and half at home, why not?'

Most of the customers, especially the older local residents, come in 'as regular as clockwork', says Pet. There are certain people, if I don't see them I'll ring them, or go round and knock on the door. There's a seventy-one year old lady who comes in a couple of times a week – not to wash always, but for a chat. She is here spot-on 9am. She'll come down over those hills, even in the snow.' If she's not coming, Pet will get a phone call. Pet describes herself as 'a bit of a counsellor really. People come in with their problems, about their husbands or wives.' Customers treat Pet as if she knows everything and everyone: 'While they're picking up the dry cleaning they'll ask "how shall I sew this?" or "where can I buy that?"' Pet's proud of doing a good job and giving

good advice. She knows that fabrics are much more particular these days, and that 'Do Not Tumble Dry' means just that, but she didn't manage to stop the customer 'who put expensive football kit in the tumble dryer for too long and it burnt!'

Occasionally Pet has to take charge of some surprising situations. She once came in to find that 'two of them were sat there, one had his hands over his boxer shorts and one had a tea towel! They were travelling around the world and decided to wash everything, even their shoes.' She's now prepared for that; 'If someone comes in and starts taking a few items off I go "Whoa! No further than your vest!"'

As to the future, Pet thinks that although there will always be a need for launderettes, it might be a dying trade. 'The ones that are open will stay open, but you never see a new one opening.'

# FAIRFIELD ROAD TO MOUNT PLEASANT TERRACE 80-70

# CHAPTER 27

**A** present day shopper walking along this stretch of the street won't need a bag, as all six shops in the terrace are currently either unused or providing services other than food retail. The terrace was built around 1905, offering shoppers fish and groceries, as well as a music shop and the Bristol Steam Carpet Beating Company. Later occupants in the terrace included Madame de Ville, a milliner and Thomas Cassels, a surgeon. A local resident describes the doctor's surgery in the 1920s, 'the windows were painted black and you couldn't see inside how many patients were waiting.'

In the 1960s, Chiswell's radio engineers operated from 78 and next door was Broadmead Ltd, dealing in the same business. The latter, at one time describing itself as 'England's largest radio retailers', was a branch of the company set up by the Bedminster-born philanthropist, John James. Broadmead Ltd later became electrical dealers Civic Stores and at some point was a branch of Currys. In the 1960s and 70s there was clearly enough demand to sustain several radio, and later TV, dealers in North Street. In addition, Bristol East Radio and Valevision operated from premises almost opposite. Valerie Wood, who set up and ran Valevision with her husband, recalls the congenial relations between the various operations: 'Bristol East Radio were great friends. Right

Taxi drivers at Club Cars (78), 2014

opposite was Chiswell's who was another radio and TV shop. He would come over to us in the morning and there would be Mark and 'Chissie', as we would call him, all having coffee.

The closure of Chiswell's, which also sold records, is recalled by Valerie: 'When Mr Chiswell died, his wife asked us if we wanted to buy [the business]. We went and looked and it wanted so much doing to it. So they sold it to the Conservative Party and they had it as their headquarters.'

At some point the two end shops (72 and 70) were re-faced in Bath stone, probably when the Somerset and Wiltshire Trustees Savings Bank opened a branch here in the late 1920s. David Levy had previously run a pawnbrokers shop here. The bank later became a branch, now closed, of the National Savings Bank.

Mrs Bishop's pre-War music shop at number 74 was taken over as a branch of Duck, Son & Pinker in 1944. The image is from a brochure published in 1948 to celebrate the centenary of the business. The Bath-based company closed in 2011, but many a Bristol piano still bears this name, and in their heyday the company estimated that it tuned an average of 1,250 pianos per week

# MOUNT PLEASANT TERRACE TO GREVILLE STREET 68-50

**CHAPTER 28**

**B**eer from Mrs Bridgett's Greville House off-licence seems to have been the only purchase possible for shoppers when this row was built around 1900, but by 1907, much of the residential terrace had been converted into shops. Walter Todd sold 'cycles and phonographs', Willway's Dye Works had a depot here and fish and fruit were also on offer.

A few local people remember this parade when there were still plenty of food shops, but change was underway: the corner shop (68) owned by the grocer Pullins had, by the 1950s, expanded next door and become a much-loved local florists. Roy Pullin [not related] recalls: 'Pullins the Florist was run by Mrs Pullin and her son Royston. There is no doubt that Jenkins in East Street had the bulk of the [local] flower trade but Pullins had a good name for quality, even though they were slightly dearer.' Bob Bennett recalls this shop was very much part of the community, and how Royston Pullin's mother 'was a member of the Ebenezer Methodist Church. After she died he continued to supply flowers to the church.'

Number 60 was originally Henry Tuck's 'wet fish shop,' being taken over by George Willmott in the late 1930s and continuing to trade for at least another forty years. Bob Bennett also remembers the shop:

*I remember my grandmother buying fish there, they sold all types. We lived with my grandmother and before I went to school she would take me shopping and on the fishmonger's slab was a big piece of marble top the full width of the shop, with all the different sorts of fish – the yellows, the whites, the greys. At the back of the shop they sold things like potatoes and vegetables.*

Muriel and Ken Eley also recall the shop, with its open front: 'All they had were steel shutters. They would put the shutters up and [they] would be open.'

Mrs Hilda Plucknett was licensee at the time of this 1950s photo. The off-licence (50) was at the corner of Greville Street. Almost opposite in Braunton Road was the Plucknett vinegar and ginger beer factory. Captain Plucknett was conductor of the orchestra at Ebenezer Chapel's Bedminster Brotherhood

All the shops once selling food stuffs, with the exception of Oriental Chef (64) have gone, now offering other services including upholsterers, In Recovery, and Victoria Jane, hairdressers, where net curtains provide a degree of privacy for customers.

# 56 AND 58 SECONDADDRESS AND IN RECOVERY

**Numbers 56 and 58 were originally occupied by a painting and decorating business; later, a register office 'for servants'.** Ken Whitehead recalls his father, a builder and decorator, opening a hardware shop here in 1934. Ken was born in Greville Street and his father, Harold Whitehead continued the business at number 56 until the late 1950s. By 1962 the shop and its neighbour were operating as one, firstly Edgell's Wholesale Tobacconists, then in the 1970s, as Goodall's, selling gold, antiques and jewellery.

Emma Williams and her husband Dave are two of many new entrepreneurs along North Street. As local residents they wanted to set up in business nearby, in 2005 opening Fanatic Scooters in numbers 56 and 58. Specialising in imported

Emma Williams of In Recovery (56), 2013

Lambretta and Vespa scooters, they soon attracted 'customers from all along the M4 corridor and down the M5.' Like some of the other specialist shops along the road, trade on Saturdays outstripped the rest of the week combined. Much of their stock was imported from India, and they even wrote the 'Indian Lambretta Guide'. Business did well, but then the combination of rising shipping prices, the exchange rate of the rupee, and the recession meant they had to close the shop side of the business.

Not daunted, Emma and Dave have converted the shop into two businesses, SecondAddress and In Recovery, the latter run by Emma. Emma says she has always been quite practical, so after Fanatic Scooters closed she went to college and learnt upholstery. After studying for two years she now runs a successful business restoring chairs, footstools and similar items, as well as making cushions and lampshades. She also works on her own pieces to sell and usually has plenty to do on commission. Emma is very adaptable: if a piece of furniture needs a basic varnish first, she's quite happy for the customer to do that themselves, or she can do the whole job, including, as she says, 'the internal rickety stuff and show-wood.' But if you want 'shabby-chic' she can do that too.

Every new customer has been recommended by a previous customer or has been walking past and seen the eye-catching shop window display with items in their 'before and after' state to show the improvements that can be made to a tired piece of furniture. Emma truly believes a good reputation is going to be her main form of advertising.

# 54 VICTORIA JANE, LADIES' HAIRDRESSER

**'Mrs Blackburn at the ironmongers, Mr and Mrs Loxton, the lady who worked in Goodall's, the wife of the butcher up the road' – Jane Hawkins can list at least a dozen local shopkeepers whose hair she regularly cut and permed since she opened Victoria Jane over thirty years ago.** Her father was a chauffeur for Wills' and her mother worked for Hilda Geller who ran the hairdressers here, which is why Jane's parents lived over the shop. Later on, Jane started her apprenticeship in Keynsham with a skilled hairdresser 'who had trained with André Bernard.' Jane explained how when Mrs Geller decided to retire she jokingly asked her parents if they would like to set her up in business and so, aged just twenty, Jane took over the shop and the customer goodwill that went with it.

This 'goodwill' comprised many loyal female customers, among who were Wills' pensioners. Jane started the shop just as Wills' was closing, but says that she 'didn't notice the change in trade as much as others, because in my case the people that I dealt with were already retired.' Talking of her clients, Jane says, 'I suppose we've grown older together. Some of them have been coming ever since I started the business, for example, one is aged ninety and she used to work in Pullins the florist along the road. They did my bouquet when I got married.'

Jane's clients may have got older with her ('I've seen the Wills' ladies come, and unfortunately go, too'), but the styles have hardly changed at all. Jane prides herself on her skills and how she meets the needs of 'the mature client.' All her sinks are front-facing, for comfort and safety, she says, not the back-wash sinks to be found in most salons today. Her assistant didn't think there were many places that do perms now, and Jane agreed:

*I do perms and proper what we call old-fashioned 'wave sets'. I can do the traditional stuff for my mature age group. My oldest client is ninety nine and until recently she came into the salon, but now I visit her at home. At ninety nine years of age watching her using a mobile under a drier was hilarious!*

When Jane started up she worked flat out, opening Monday to Saturday, and when she got married she 'lived over the shop as it was easy to work six days a week when it was just downstairs.' For

Although the shutters are down, Jane Hawkins' hairdressers is very much open for business. 2014

her mature clients, 'Christmas is one of the busiest times of the year, and Easter, they get ready to have their Easter perms.'

Even though Jane's style hasn't altered much, the hairdressing trade in the street has changed a great deal: 'When I started there were two hairdressers, Sally by the zebra crossing and Shirley in the fish and chip shop. I could nip over the road to Shirley and say I've run out of whatever, and that would be fine.' There are many more hairdressers now in North Street, and Jane fears that the competitiveness has led to what she notices as the very high turnover of businesses. Not that Jane is worried about her own trade. She doesn't need to advertise: 'It's word

of mouth, but most of my clients are regulars. I have a client who comes all the way from Thornbury and one from Australia – when she's in the country. I like to think we bring a bit more personal touch, care, making sure the clients are warm, for example, and have a cup of tea. '

Her clients agree with Jane when she says, 'It's a nice friendly business. I think my clients would say it is cosy, perhaps more personal, people ringing up to see how you are.' Until this year, Jane and some of her clients used to go out for a Christmas meal, 'a trip out of Bristol to a country pub, for example. They love it, up to twenty five of us!' That loyalty has been two-way, ever since recent circumstances have meant Jane has not been able to open the shop as often. But she says she is 'made of sturdy stuff, and is loyal to her clients, keeping the shop open whenever I can and the clients have stuck by me in these difficult times too.' The shop is now open for part of the week, and on one day she visits her clients who can no longer make it to North Street.

Jane describes how much busier the street was when she started: 'On a Saturday morning you literally couldn't walk down the pavement, you had to step into the gutter it was so busy.' Jane is not optimistic about the future of the street. She thinks the number of offices has made a big difference and that 'the soul of Bedminster has gone, and another nail in the coffin will be residents' parking.' But for her own salon, she feels that the loyalty of her clients makes it 'a nice steady business,' and she is happy with 'the way things tick over.'

# GREVILLE STREET TO LANGTON PARK 48-40

# CHAPTER 29

**T**his rank of five shops was built in the early 1870s, at the same time as the two side roads at either end. It replaced two older houses facing North Street, both of which had orchards running up the hillside behind. At this time the shops included a baker, a bootmaker, grocers and a coffee tavern. This practical mix changed little over the following fifty years. Just before the Second World War, number 48 became Bollom of Bristol, dyers and cleaners (**see 237**), providing a laundry collection service. John Lenthall, who ran the furniture shop on the other side of North Street (**see 45-47**), remembers Sam Bollom in the post-war period, when John's firm delivered furniture to the Bollom's home in Long Ashton.

## 44 LOXTON'S, SPORTS OUTFITTERS
(NOW LEVEL CUTS, BARBERS)

 By the 1950s, the furniture dealer at number 44 had gone, the shop becoming Loxton's Sports Outfitters. Gerry Loxton was a popular man, remembered by many local residents. As Malcolm Pearce said:

*He was everybody's idea of a sports master. We started up the Ashton*

## 40 WILLIAMS, HOSIERY
(NOW BARBERS)

Edgar Williams, hosiery manufacturer, who operated from the corner shop (40) is a reminder of how at one time, businesses were able to expand by calling on the services of family members. Edgar was one of thirteen children of Henry Williams, who had set up as a knitwear manufacturer at number 73, the knitting being done by members of the family. Henry's son Joshua then went on to run his

father's business, while Edgar ran the business at number 40 in the 1920s. Other examples of expansion of local family-run shop businesses include the Butt's, Knowle's, Pople's, Luton's and Collard's, each of whom ran several branches both in North Street and elsewhere in Bristol.

Another of Henry's children, Edith, married Gilbert Robbins who ran a North Street cobblers (**see 95**). Their son, also Gilbert, described how the knitting machines were operated in the window, producing men's and lady's socks, stockings and jerseys. It proved a great attraction for passers-by, including Gilbert who promptly 'fell for Edith' who was working in the window at the time!

*Wanderers Football and he supplied the kit. After weeks of talk about what colour kit we'd have, he came back with yellow shirts with a white collar. When we told him we didn't want that, he said they'd have to do as they were on special offer! If you wanted anything sporty Loxton's was where you went – you didn't go into town. I bought a pair of football boots there and they were one of the first to come out with screw-in studs.*

According to Gina Stamford, Gerry Loxton 'was a very nice man, nothing was too much trouble and he would get you whatever you wanted. He was a short man and had a moustache. I bought my roller skate boots from him and my swimsuits.' Frank Phillips also remembers how helpful Gerry Loxton was. 'If you had a problem he would sort it out. I bought my first set of darts there, the stems and flights. I also bought my only judo suit from him.'

A keen cricketer, Bob Bennett remembers being taken to Loxton's by his father to buy his first cricket gear. 'I played mainly amateur at church – we had our own cricket team and we'd play anybody.' Ken Summerill recalls that 'we used to buy our Scout and Cub uniforms there.' Steve Williamson thinks that Mr Loxton 'tended to employ school lads, but they didn't last long because as soon as they reached 18 and wanted higher wages they tended to leave. Although Loxton's expanded in the 1960s by extending into number 42, by the 1990s it had gone out of business.

## CHAPTER 30
# LANGTON PARK TO MERRYWOOD ROAD 38-14

**T**he development of this stretch is similar to other sections of North Street: cottages and larger houses along a country road were replaced by terraces of buildings, mainly shops, in a burst of development between 1880 and 1900 as Bristol underwent a period of rapid expansion. Maps show that at the beginning of Queen Victoria's reign this stretch of North Street was fronted by an orchard and just two or three buildings. By the 1880s, the newly-built Langton Park had been constructed, part of the development of the nearby suburb of Southville. The row finished at the much older Bull Lane which later became Merrywood, then Merrywood Lane and finally Merrywood Road, the name which has remained.

From the corner of Langton Park, a terrace of five shops was built eastwards along North Street. It was named Peartree Terrace, no doubt a reference to the nearby orchard. The first shops here were a confectioner, china dealer, wardrobe dealer and fancy stores, tobacconist and the Peartree bakery. Further along, one of the older houses, Balkan House, remained, but the development then continued eastwards with more shops as far as the corner of North Street and Merrywood Lane. By the 1890s, the whole stretch had been fully developed, every building being a shop and offering a wide choice of fried fish, boots, trunks, secondhand clothes, baskets and meat, as well as having a haircut. The outfitters, Keith Pople Ltd, had a branch at number 20 (**see 227-231**).

## 38 AND 34 WU AND BING, LAUNDRIES
(NOW AVON NEWS, NEWSAGENTS AND KWAN'S, CHINESE TAKEAWAY)

**The shop on the corner of Langton Park and North Street was originally a confectioners, but the Wing Chung laundry opened here in the 1920s.** By 1930 this business had become the Cah Kee Laundry, but they then moved over to the other side of North Street not long afterwards (**see 29**). 1956 must have been a 'clean' year in North Street, as the business Wu and Bing not only took over the Cah Kee laundry but also opened a branch at number 34. However both their new branches lasted only a few years, only the shop at number 34 remaining. Ken and Muriel Eley recall how it 'did a lot of work for the hospitals – sheets and laundry.' Roy

Pullin remembers using their services:

*In the days when separate collars were the norm, we always had our collars laundered at the Chinese Laundry. The collars used to come back glazed and coiled ready to fit around your neck. No other laundry could match them for finish. I remember they were all marked on the inside with a Chinese cipher. Goodness knows how the laundry kept everyone's collars separate.*

Doreen Hamblin also remembers the same shop: 'I was working for the Tramway as a bus conductress. We would not go to work in those days in casual dress – we were compelled to wear uniform. I always had my white shirts and collars laundered at the Chinese Laundry in North Street, almost opposite The Rex.'

When Wu and Bing closed in the early 1970s, the shop became Mak's Fried Fish Shop, currently Kwan's Kitchen and Fish Bar. The opening of a 'Chinese laundry' here in the 1950s, and its later conversion to a fish bar, reflects national changes of the time: this period saw a big increase in Britain's Chinese population, mainly immigrants from Hong Kong. Not long afterwards, the availability of domestic washing machines hastened the demise of high street laundries across the country.

Number 36 originally traded as a china dealer. Before the war it was taken over by Mrs Alice Smith who ran a toy shop there until the late 1950s. 'It was absolutely packed with toys,' remembers Joan Marsh, 'and Dad would buy us the 6d Rupert books. It was a very small shop, and it used to have dolls hanging from the ceiling. My dad took me in there to buy me my favourite doll.'

The newsagent on the corner with Langton Park is currently Avon News (38). Number 36 (here Stuckeys) opened in 2014 as Margot May, a 'retro' tea shop, run by Jenny Smith and her team: "The first time I walked down and got to the Spotted Cow I was wondering if it was really the same street I'd heard so much about. But we did some more research and realised it was the right place for us." The poster reading 'Every Bubble's Passed Its Fizzical', and the trousers, date this picture to c1976

## 30 WYATT AND ACKERMAN LTD

**Behind this modest shop front lies a thriving business which supplies companies throughout the UK.** The owner and Managing Director is Martyn Lewis who describes the development of the business:

*Les Wyatt was the founder of this company in 1950 and in 1989 my father and his brother bought the business from Les. Originally it was a small company covering just 80 to100 miles around Bristol, supplying packaging and stationery – up to Evesham, down to Ivybridge, over to Wales. I'm still going to people in South Wales that Les Wyatt delivered to 60 years ago. My father kept the name because it was well known. [He] died in 1997. I was 23 and kept things going, then in 1998 I took it on from my mother and uncle.*

*We deal with some big companies which we've got because of our name – Pizza Hut, Carpet Right, Bristol City Football Club, and the NHS. We're quite diverse, in that we supply the small shop down the road with stationery and packaging and also big concerns, like supplying till rolls to the shops at the London Olympic Games!*

**123**

Managing Director of Wyatt & Ackerman, Martyn Lewis, cutting packs of greaseproof paper on the company's Patent Furnivale guillotine. The paper is resold for wrapping fish and chips. The guillotine is undated, but similar models come from the Victorian era. 2014

Some of the staff from the shop and behind the scenes. L to R: Suzanne Green; Martyn Lewis; Andrea Woodhouse; Helen Lippiatt; Debby Taylor; Joan Nurmeleht. 2014

In spite of this, the firm maintains strong links with local customers.

*The old tale is that it would be a day's work for the van to get from one end of North Street to the other to supply all the shops on our list. If you come to us you can buy everything you need to start up your business. We've always done well and have branched out and gone more corporate. Our new website is aimed at attracting companies with 10 or 15 stores, but at the same time we will supply a shop like the Lion Stores. Although we market ourselves, we get a lot of business on recommendation. I've never ever thought of changing the name. We have 8,500 square feet in total, retail downstairs, offices upstairs, cash and carry out the back and warehousing. We employ 14 people.*

Given the amount of stock which the company sells, Martyn Lewis has sometimes considered renting a larger warehouse nearby, but decided against it.

*A lot of the goods we supply go direct from the manufacturers so there's no additional cost, which has saved spending out on a warehouse. We cover the whole of the UK up to Inverness, to Cornwall, Swansea, Ipswich, the Channel Islands, Northern and Southern Ireland. We can work on lower margins because there are no additional overheads.*

Martyn concludes: 'To be honest for the first ten-fifteen years the shop ran itself; then I realised how important the shop is to North Street. Bedminster is a very close knit community. Ultimately I like supplying the shops in North Street, you have to support each other.'

# 28 THE AQUATIC STORE

**This shop is 'Definitely Different' as its signboard announces, with its humid atmosphere and 130 tanks of tropical fish.** Owner Steve Chivers started up the business in 2010 after the shop had been empty for over two years. Steve's shop assistant, Martin explained that 'it seemed like an up and coming area, a lot of new businesses opening up down this end, a good time to get in. It's a brand new business. I've always had a passion for fish.' It is this expert knowledge that is clearly what has brought the shop such a good reputation. Steve says that what is special is that he offers 'absolutely, customer service'. He is an expert in the field, and he and Martin have both kept fish since they were youngsters.

As a specialist shop, their customers come from far and wide: 'Ninety nine percent of our customers don't come from Bedminster. They come from all over Bristol, from Cardiff, Manchester and even Scotland. It does tend to be more men than women, but we also get youngsters coming in with their parents. Steve imports all his own fish. As he says:

*They get flown in to Heathrow once a week. It is a well-regulated industry. Every crate on the plane gets looked at, partly because of drugs being brought in, but Defra [Department for Environment, Food and Rural Affairs] are there too, checking for smuggled species that are banned from import.*

The puffer fish he has on display is 'a rescue fish, from Defra. It was seized as part of a consignment that had illegal imports.' Steve has some quite rare species in the shop, including a Fly River turtle. Business has grown since they opened, and he thinks prospects seem very good. Steve and Martin say: 'We had to expand out the back and we haven't got enough room!' Steve advertises in *Practical Fishkeeping*, but the rest of his marketing is by word of

Steve Chivers (left) and Martin Chamberlain of The Aquatic Store (28), 2014

mouth. There are one or two well-known customers, but he is keeping quiet about that, suffice it to say that 'a Bristol City player could be walking through the door sometime!'

The atmosphere in the shop is calm, each customer being offered expert advice, even over the smallest purchase of a pack of fish food. It feels like a club of enthusiasts, welcoming beginners and experts alike.

## 26 MRS E THOMAS, GREENGROCERS
(NOW AURAURA, GIFT SHOP)

 **In 1922 the Thomas family started a greengrocery at number 26.** George Thomas describes the business, run by his grandfather and grandmother:

*As a boy I paid many visits and was*

very proud of the lone word 'Thomas' above the door. I was always being given fruit of one sort or another and the lovely fruity smell of the shop was a delight. I used to see Grandad in the parlour up a small flight of steps from the shop. We had a pet parrot in the corner who wasn't short of a word or three! Grandad was a retired engine driver who did the run from Bristol to Penzance. He had rail engine pictures all round the room to remind him of the good old days. He and Grandma had two helpers in the shop. One was Reg Porter a son by Gran's first marriage. The other was Nellie Mildren, her maiden name was Masters so I am informed. She was the daughter of the owner of a local shoe shop Masters [34]. Whether the two were married or not I'm not sure but no one would bat an eyelid these days.*

John Walker has fond memories of the shop and the other nearby greengrocers when he was younger:

*I lived in Langton Park and as a young lad was often sent there by my mum to buy potatoes and so on. I can picture Reg Porter well, he had dark wavy hair tinged with grey and a rather sharp nose. He would always be joking with customers. Interestingly at that time there were four greengrocers' shops within a hundred yards of each other. A few shops along in the direction of Langton Park was Pursey's then a little further up North Street was Wilmott's. On the other side on the corner of Braunton Road was Saunder's.*

The family name continued over the shop until the late 1950s, the shop continuing as a greengrocers until the mid-1960s.

Aileen James' (nee Bosley) father at the family's drapers shop in Redcliffe Hill

# 22 BOSLEY'S OF BEDMINSTER, LADIES' OUTFITTERS

(NOW JAMAICAN DINER, RESTAURANT)

**Aileen Bosley was a young child when the family shop of Bosley's, Drapers and Outfitters on Redcliffe Hill was bombed during the Second World War.** Her father had to move out and found suitable premises at 16 North Street, on the corner of Merrywood Road, where he could continue in business. In times of austerity during and just after the war, shopkeepers such as Mr. Bosley were keen to offer anything that was in demand and so customers were not only able to buy

their clothes and accessories here, but other items such as linoleum. As post-war business grew, the business expanded in the late 1950s to a shop three doors away at number 22, which specialized in ladies' lingerie.

Like many shop-keeping families, Aileen and her parents lived above the shop. Her school friend, Joan Payne, who lived opposite above Pitt the Bakers (**see 9**), recalls some of the finer niceties of the two sides of the street: 'We were Bedminster, and they [the Bosleys] were Southville. Aileen and I used to look at each other through the window across the road and wave and blow on the window and write on it, but we weren't allowed to play together!'

Aileen attended nearby Southville Primary School. As a child she was often given the tasks of tidying and

sorting behind the scenes at the family shop. Little did she realise then that years later, as a teenager with thoughts of a teaching career, she would in fact become a successful businesswoman. Her mother, who ran the 'ladies' shop' (22) unfortunately suffered a stroke while at work and her father retired from the business not long after, in the early 1970s, to look after his wife. The family then closed the shop at number 16, but Aileen carried on as manager of number 22. Fortunately she inherited two experienced members of staff, taking on others over the years, who she trained up to be 'fitters'. Her father let her manage the entire business and trade thrived.

In her early days as manager, Aileen's regular customers were still a mixture of very loyal, older people, and the passing trade of the 'Wills' Girls', even though the Wills' factories were in the process of moving out of the immediate area. Unlike some shops, Aileen did not stay open late, but her regular weekday and Saturday opening, with Wednesday half-day closing, sufficed to build up trade and a good reputation. Bosley's of Bedminster became known as the place to go to have fitted lingerie, in time becoming main agent for Playtex & Triumph ladies' underwear. Aileen recalls the Playtex sales representative telling her that she sold more of one particular line in her shop than in Debenham's in central Bristol. Customers would be measured and fitted in the changing rooms out the back, then collecting their boxed purchases from shelves behind the counter. It was all very discreet, Aileen says, with no labels on the purchases as they left the shop.

Much of the stock was kept under the counter in a set of glass-topped units with drawers beneath. Aileen remembers that Christmas was a good time for trade, when the shop would also stock toys. Presents for women needed buying, of course, and men took the plunge to come in for gifts for their wives or girlfriends, although all too often these were returned shortly after Christmas for a more accurate size!

As well as lingerie the shop sold various accessories and, for a time, did a good line in knitting yarn. However Aileen recalls that this was hit by the introduction of VAT on wool, which meant that 'knitting your own' was not much cheaper than buying a ready-made garment.

By now the family was no longer living upstairs and in common with several other North Street shop-owners in this period, older members of the Bosley family had moved to nearby Long Ashton. Aileen would be at the shop most days, to ensure its smooth running, but with the responsibilities of a young family she was very much the shop manager. She recalls having three or so women working part-time for her. Aileen put great trust in her staff, which in turn was met with loyalty and long service.

For a while Aileen's neighbouring shop (20) was a branch of Keith Pople, outfitters. However there was no rivalry as Pople's specialised in children's clothing. Aileen and her husband would meet other shop owners at the local Traders' Association. Aileen remembers an example of this local camaraderie in recalling a nearby shopkeeper, who ran a second-hand audio shop. At this time, in the 1990s, Aileen was having 'a spot of bother' with local youths. With Aileen's female staff feeling occasionally intimidated by young men peering into the shop, a bell-push concealed under the counter brought a rapid response from the burly shop keeper next door and trouble was quickly averted on more than one occasion.

Because of its position, Aileen felt that their shop was like an extended part of East Street. Her customers were mainly local, but she also had people, some, no doubt, former Wills' workers, who came by bus from Hartcliffe to do their shopping in East Street. Aileen continued to adapt to the times, but by the 1990s shopping habits had started to change. She still had her loyal older customers but passing trade had diminished. Supermarkets were selling underwear and the idea of a bespoke, fitted lingerie service was perhaps seen by an increasing number of women as antiquated, unnecessary or just time-consuming. Now retired, Aileen sees that 'personalised shopping' is back again, as a thriving niche market in certain products.

Aileen Bosley's shop, from her album. Undated

'Poet's Corner' at 14 North Street, at the junction with Merrywood Road. The gargoyle is often said to be of the Poet Laureate Robert Southey, whose grandfather's house was nearby

# 14 'POETS' CORNER'
(NOW TAYLORS ESTATE AGENTS)

A glance up above the door of this corner shop reveals an eroded bust with the inscription 'Poets' Corner 1882'. The celebratory bust is said to have been erected by Aldred (sometimes known as Alfred) Daw Collard, a butcher who lived a few yards away, who also built this and other properties nearby. The Collard family business is better remembered for their shop further along North Street on the opposite side (**see 57**), which was run by Aldred's cousin Alfred. Aldred was a well-known local entrepreneur, butcher and poet, described in *Southville People and Places*:

*Aldred Collard had done a fair amount of travelling and it was known in his circle that he placed a huge variety of foreign coins under the foundations of the first house he built. His favourite pastime was reading poetry and something of a poet himself, he erected the gargoyle over his corner shop. The premises were used at one time as a meeting place for miners.*

Some of the poet-butcher's work was published, having been sold in his shop for 1d, all proceeds going to the Bristol hospitals. This is an example of his work, now less well-known than that of his hero Robert Southey who also knew this part of North Street in earlier times:

> *Who is there alive who has not been to town,*
> *Or walked along streets where the rails are laid down,*
> *But has seen tram-cars, so lofty and bright –*
> *Fitted with splendour and illuminated at night –*
> *Also noticed the horses, so used to the track,*
> *And don't know the sound of their clickety clack?*

Another of his works was entitled 'The Redcliffe and Bedminster Christmas Meat Show of 1885' and named the twenty-six butchers shops between North Street and Redcliffe Hill.

Aldred Collard came to live in this stretch of North Street around 1874, settling in Enmore House. His only neighbour then was John Peter Heeremans, nurseryman of nearby Pear Tree Gardens. Collard was actively developing the area as a house builder and must have decided to sell the land fronting North Street, because seven years later the stretch of shops called Peartree Terrace was built and Collard had moved around the corner to Redcliff House in Merrywood Lane. It seems that his new front and side gardens were part of the same pear orchard, now mostly built on, that was once tended by Mr Heeremans. Some of the orchard land still remains, hidden behind the shops and houses which make up this row.

# MERRYWOOD ROAD
## TO BOOTH ROAD 12-2

**R**eaders following this trail along North Street on foot, not from the comfort of a chair, can celebrate the end of their walk with suitable refreshments in the Steam Crane. Built on the site of an older coaching inn, this prominent pub is sandwiched between a row of three shops, a workshop and a stylish 1913 former doctor's surgery.

The north side of the street, looking towards Pen Corner (the white building in the distance) and Merrywood Road. Beyond is a Belisha Beacon, still in use. The laundry is now Kwan's Fish Bar (34). Just visible is the entrance into the much older building behind number 30 (currently Wyatt & Ackerman). c1945-55

## 12 PEN CORNER
(NOW EDWARD'S, ESTATE AGENTS)

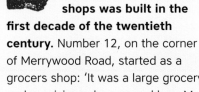 **The short row of three shops was built in the first decade of the twentieth century.** Number 12, on the corner of Merrywood Road, started as a grocers shop: 'It was a large grocery and provisions shop owned by a Mr Gingell, where one could take a basin and buy treacle or jam for 2d or 3d.

They had rows of tins of biscuits with glass lids and you could select a few from each to make up a pound of mixed biscuits.'

The Gingell business closed in the 1940s. In 1955, Peter Budd who, at the time was running a newsagents in Long Ashton, decided to take over the lease of the shop. It was trading as CJ Kiff, being run by the Bristol ballpoint pen company Tallon, who used it to test out the saleability of their products. Peter also took

on the employees, 'in their smart blue overalls,' who taught him the business:

*It was very quiet in the early days. We used to take about £5 on a Wednesday morning. I modernised the stock and it was just at the time when the greeting card market was starting, so I built up that side. Fortunately there were three to four thousand girls in Will's and Robinson's nearby and they always wanted to buy the largest and most flamboyant cards*

Opposite Poet's Corner was Peter Budd's shop (12), which he named Pen Corner. Undated

*for their boyfriend! 'I want a card for me chap with a lotta glitter on! 'He do love me true.'' At Christmas we turned over the back rooms to trade, with a large table with six boxes divided into 1d, 2d and so on cards. There was always a good sale of pens for italic writing, which was all the rage in schools at that time. The pens in those days were, of course, the top Parker 51, Waterman's and Platignum. We had glass display cases with all the pens on show. When there was a leaving present at Wills', a girl would invariably come in and buy a gold plated Parker 51. A Parker 51 in those days was £5 and my profit £1, so I judged everything I had to buy in my life on how many 51s I had to sell to afford it!*

'Pens were on the left as you walked in,' Peter remembers, 'Quink ink, stationery, greetings cards and paperbacks were on the right hand side.' Later on he introduced Meccano, Hornby, and Dinky toys. 'In 1953, I sold quite a lot of Coronation sets – the coach and horses. Afterwards I couldn't give them away, and now they're worth a fortune!'

To celebrate John Atyeo's retirement from Bristol City Football Club in 1966, Peter filled the window with photographs of John Atyeo. 'I put a couple of footballs in and some kit.' A few people still recall these displays, as Malcolm Pearce describes: 'They had an exhibition, just after John Atyeo had just played for England against Brazil. They had a mannequin with a Brazilian shirt, a photo of John and his England cap. It was wonderful to go and look at it at night when it was lit up. That was about 1957.' Another Bristol City fan recalls real-life contact with Atyeo: 'I spotted him coming out of Pen Corner and rushed over with my mates to get close to our hero. Although he was probably very busy, he didn't hesitate to stop, sign autographs and chat. If a friend hadn't dragged him away I reckon John would have popped into Dean Lane Park with us for a kick about!'

In common with a number of North Street shopkeepers of this period, Peter lived in nearby Long Ashton rather than above the premises. In spite of living outside Bristol, Peter was still very involved in the life of the area:

*It was a little community between the shopkeepers, right the way up to the Hen and Chicken. I was in that lower half, very much linked to Cannon Street, and East Street was the prime place in Bristol before Broadmead got going. It was only when Wills' went it started to deteriorate. You can't imagine how different it was.*

Peter was also a leading member of the local Rotary Club. In the south Bristol floods of 1968 the Club established a relief fund. 'We raised something like £30,000 and Miles [EN Miles in nearby Cannon Street] gave us blankets, pillows and sheets at cost

This 1900 plan proposed 'two houses and dwelling places to be erected' between number 12 (later Pen Corner) and the Star Inn. They (8 and 10) were built almost to plan, although the observant will notice the window order is reversed

The next shop (10) opened as a 'chemist and druggist', run by James Allen when it was built in the early 1900s. A few years later the business was taken over by Walter Dunford and the pharmacy trade continued here when Hedley Price took over after the Second World War. The Price family also owned shops further up North Street **(see 244-246)**.

# 8 BLACKBURN'S, IRONMONGERS

(NOW NUMBER 8 NORTH STREET, FURNITURE SHOP)

 **The final shop in this parade began as a corn and forage merchants.** By 1910 the premises was being shared with Charles Blackburn, ironmongers, and that business continued trading from here for at least sixty years. Alan Walker recalls the shop:

*The name of Blackburn the ironmonger was very well known. I remember him well – he kept a very well stocked shop of what is known now as DIY Goods, in those days if you wanted two or three screws etc, that's what you bought not a packet of ten. Mr Blackburn was not a very big man, with sandy colour hair and sharp eyes. I believe he used to be a magistrate.*

Frank Phillip describes Blackburn's as being 'like Lion Stores **(see 219)** but bigger. It sold screws and nails by the quarter pound. You could buy almost anything.' Carole Hawkes remembers 'being sent by my dad to Blackburn's for a pound of nails weighed into a brown bag,' and Bob Bennett also recalls being

price. Hector Tanner in West Street supplied hundreds of electric kettles. We raised the money and distributed it to the [relief] centres.'

Peter describes the period when he took over the shop as 'the glorious upturn from [post-war] austerity – the first foreign holidays, the first car owners.' The greetings card side of the business grew quickly and Peter's company expanded. 'I opened the third specialist greeting card shop in

Baldwin Street [The Card Centre]. But Pen Corner was probably my favourite. I went between the two and eventually ended up with three or four shops.' As Peter explains, this success was followed by a slump in business, 'when the axe fell and Wills' moved to Hartcliffe. Overnight the girls spending 10/- were gone and their mothers spending 6d were left.' He hung on for a while, eventually selling the premises in the 1970s.

a customer: 'I used to be sent there to get our paraffin for our heaters. You'd take your can and they'd draw it off from a pump on the counter. He sold hardware things as well.' Dave Russell recalls its 'solid wooden floor, and it always used to smell of turpentine and paraffin.'

In more recent times the shop traded as the Nylon Shop, much loved by bargain-hunters for fabrics of every description. A somewhat misleading name – although nylon could be purchased there – the shop had the appearance of a jumble sale, but hid many gems, such as fur fabric, material for fancy dress and pantomime costumes, as well as reels of cotton and pieces of foam. Most notable was the welcome, as Roy Gallop recalls: 'Oh yes, we used it a lot. The old lady was a bit fierce. If you went in and asked "Do you do knitting?" she'd say "I certainly don't", not "Oh no, but you could get them at so and so."'

(Top) The rank of shops between the Star and Merrywood Road was built c1900-1910. Ironmonger Charles Blackburn was there from the start, and the business at number 8 was open for over sixty years. In this picture buckets are 1/6d and large bins for ashes are 4/11d. Charging is available for the heavy glass batteries used in valve radios

(Bottom) Number 8, now the Nylon Shop. Under the red paint, there is a ghost image of the word 'Ironmongers.' When the shop closed down c2010, another complete Blackburn ironmongers signboard was discovered and preserved during its renovation

Taken in or before 1976, Blackburn's ironmongery is still in business. The pub has echoes of the former 18th century building it replaced, but with only one gable end it is quite asymmetrical

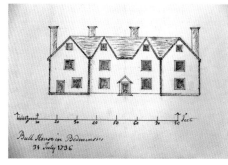

Builder's plan for Bull House, dated 31 July 1736. Accompanying papers list the quantities of timber and other building materials required. The symmetry and twin gable ends are in the style of a manor house of an earlier period, though there is nothing to suggest that it replaced such a building

# 4 – 6 THE STEAM CRANE

The current building was constructed during the closing years of the nineteenth century, the style reminiscent of a coaching inn with an entrance through an arch leading to a small courtyard beyond. The pub is, in fact on the site of a much earlier building known as Bull House. Records show that by 1775 Bull House was referred to as the Star Hotel, or Star Inn. A short distance from the inn stood the Bedminster 'turnpike', the gate for the toll-road, so it is probable that the Star was a coaching inn. In spite of having several name changes in recent years, many locals still refer to the pub as 'The Star'.

# 2 BEDMINSTER HAND CAR WASH AND VALET CENTRE

Although the final buildings along this side of North Street, adjacent to the Steam Crane, are not shops and, at a first glance, seem relatively unimportant, they have been providing a similar range of services for nearly a hundred years. Through the entrance of the end building is a car wash. Not so long ago, motorists could have a new exhaust pipe fitted here. In the 1970s, W Heathman, motor car trimmers, operated from these premises. In the 1930s, the building housed a firm of motor body builders, and in the 1880s it seems that a wheelwright worked either here or in the courtyard of what was then the Star Hotel. Coaching inns and vehicle-making and repair go hand in hand.

Records show other smaller buildings standing here in the past, but the very last building on this side of North Street was built as a doctors' surgery in 1913, its elegant, curved frontage providing a fitting end to this tour of North Street.

2A North Street

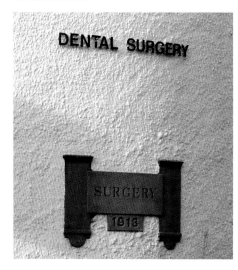

# THE STREET IS MY SHOP

**S**treet selling is a centuries-old tradition and like most high streets, North Street had, and still has, its street vendors. Phil Elliot remembers the time when Bristol had two daily papers, The Evening World and The Bristol Evening Post which prided themselves on getting the football scores into print before the supporters had got off the bus home from a City or Rovers match on a Saturday afternoon: 'There used to be a chap who sold The Evening Post with The Green'un and The Pink'un, outside the Hen and Chicken. There would be crowds of people waiting for them.'

As a paper-boy in the 1940s, Jack House remembers the newspaper vendor who ran the business:

*I did an evening paper round. I was always called upon to collect the papers from the Hen and Chicken from Freddy Kent who was quite a character. Occasionally I had the feeling that he was 'on the make' because sometimes at the end of my round I was always one or two papers short and I wasn't quite certain if that was due to a deliberate mistake. He always wore a bowler hat and he'd stand at the Hen and Chicken and shout 'Papers! Papers! Papers!' [My round] was long – Foxcote Road, Smyth Road, back up into Dampier Road – sometimes on my bicycle sometimes walking, but that wasn't the end because there was a man in Carrington Road – he was a racing enthusiast and*

Ray Bowles taking a break outside the Southville Deli (260-262). Ray sold the Evening Post from this trademark fluorescent satchel. 2014

*he always wanted the two star [edition]. In those days The Evening Post had one, two and three star, so I had to get the two star paper from Freddy Kent and make a special delivery back to the shoe repairer in Carrington Road. I did six days a week and was paid 7/6d. Straight after school, I'd dash back on my bike because people wanted their paper on time. The guy who employed me, Arthur Lewis, also delivered milk in the mornings.*

## WHEN I SOLD THE BRISTOL EVENING POST

**Ray Bowles is a familiar figure in North Street, wheeling his ancient bike with its Sturmey Archer gears and chrome headlamp as he heads for a coffee.** By the time he finished full time work in the 1980s, Ray had already taken on the role of North Street Bristol Evening Post vendor. He was born in 1919 and grew up in the then newly-built Bedminster Down council estate. His father worked on the railways, so when Ray left school at fourteen his father got him a job with him. By the outbreak of the War, Ray was a signalman and throughout the War worked in various signal boxes including a stint in one close to his house, operating the sidings into the South Liberty Lane brickyard. Ray was already selling papers before he retired: 'To tell you the truth, when I was selling The Evening Post I should have been in bed asleep, after working the night on the railway!'

After a few years selling papers outside the Hen and Chicken ('I wasn't selling much up there') Ray moved to selling The Evening Post at the Gala bingo hall further down the road: 'I'd get there about five o'clock and the van would stop – he'd run in, through the glass doors, fling the papers on the stairs and say "there you are, what you don't sell, get rid of."' Ray got into trouble when his approach to 'getting rid' of unsold papers went wrong. Every day he would wheel his bike with the unsold papers over the railway bridge across the nearby river and throw them in! He was soon found out by his employers.

At Gala Bingo, Ray would stand on the stairs to sell papers: 'They were mostly women. When they got to their favourite table there was a pile of cigarettes.' Many of the bingo players were retired Wills employees and enjoyed a free ration of cigarettes. Ray carried on selling the paper until the Gala closed down in 2008, the bingo being killed off,

so he reckons, when the smoking ban in public buildings was introduced.

Now aged 94, Ray enjoys the generosity of people in his local community, such as a trip to Strada bike shop to 'get some air in one of my tyres.'

## THE BIG ISSUE VENDOR

**Bombonica, who goes by the name Maria to make it easier for people to remember, has been selling The Big Issue on North Street since 2009.** Her 'outdoor shop' is open every day come sun or snow: 'Yes, you have to stay, whatever the weather', Maria says. On a bad day, she might only sell 'two or three, sometimes no magazines'. At busy times, such as Christmas or Easter, she will sell forty magazines in a week. She has a quota to sell and walks several miles to the Big Issue office once or twice a week to collect them. Maria doesn't meet up with other Big Issue sellers when they have get-togethers as she doesn't like drinking or smoking.

Her customers are both young and old. Some people buy the magazine weekly; others buy 'if something on the front looks special and interesting'. She reads bits of the magazine, but not much as she says she doesn't read English that well. Sometimes her children tell her what is in it.

Maria doesn't want to be selling Big Issue for ever. She wants to find cleaning or gardening work, but it's not easy as she has a family to look after,

Bombonica at her Big Issue pitch, 2013

and she thinks she doesn't speak very good English. After ten years of selling Big Issue, Maria sometimes gets upset at her prospects as she cannot afford to return to Romania to see her family. Customers are very good though and often stop and talk to her. Some people do more than just buy the magazine, and ask her if she wants a juice or a coffee: she doesn't turn them down. One of her customers has been helping her to find work, and perhaps this year will be the one when Maria can get a job she really wants to do.

## THE FLOWER SELLER

**Karen Woodley is a familiar figure outside the Brewery Theatre, selling bunches of flowers and homemade greetings cards every Thursday and Friday, weather permitting.** She gets the flowers from local growers, adding 'bits and pieces from my garden' and sells out most weeks.

# SHOPPING THROUGH THE DECADES

Peggy Triggle, whose mother and grandmother also shopped in North Street

## 1930s

### A MULTIPLICITY OF CHOICE – AND DOORSTEP SERVICE TOO!

BY PEGGY TRIGGLE

Peggy, now in her 90s, still lives in the house in Clift Road where she grew up with her sister Sheila and their parents and grandparents.

'By necessity you had to shop most days as fresh food didn't keep well and this was before the days when everyone had a 'fridge. This must have been before the war because my Grandmother did all the ordering. It was always fish on Saturdays and Grandmother would go to the fish market in town. A lot of people had their shopping delivered in those days. They came to the house; you never went to the shop. You ordered one day and it came the next. A delivery boy would ride along on a bicycle and he'd come to the door and grandma would say 'I'll have chops tomorrow', or whatever and other things. He had a list which he'd take back and deliver the chosen things the next day. Then she'd give him another list and so it went on.

Before the war, North Street had a wonderful range of shops and I remember so many of them well: Hedley Price if we needed a chemist, Stringers for haberdashery as they sold the lot! Lyes the butchers: we always used them and not Butts up the road – there were lots of butchers and everyone had their favourite. Andrew's the jewellers, where my mother and father bought me my first watch. I was about 14 or 15 and had so longed for it!

You knew everyone behind the counters. They were like friends and you knew that you could go there and get exactly what you wanted; always good service. As for being on first name terms, I'm not so sure if anyone referred to each other by first names, it would always be Mr or Mrs.

Shops were very nicely done in those days. You could do all your Christmas shopping along North Street and buy quality things, like Yardley's 'Lavender' in Hedley Price. I think it's changed because for my age I couldn't do any shopping for gifts in North Street today. Nothing would present itself to me there. It's all so different.'

Jack House, who in 1945 coaxed 7d from his mother to buy his first Clark's Pie

# 1940s AND 50s

## WHEN SHOPPING WAS A DELIGHT TO THE SENSES!

### BY JACK HOUSE

**'Anyone walking the length of North Street in the late 1940s and early 1950s would have experienced a series of sensory experiences of a unique nature – experiences which would have motivated the senses of smell, hearing and sight into overdrive.**

Beginning with unique North Street smells at the Ashton extremity, there was usually an odour emanating from the Clift House Tannery arising from the processing of animal hides. Moving up North Street a couple of hundred yards (1940s style measurement!), the odour of animal hides would be suddenly replaced by that of tobacco. This, of course, came from the various factories of WD & HO Wills situated between Greenway Bush Lane and Raleigh Road. As progression was made up North Street, two somewhat more pleasant smells became apparent. First, that of the cooking of the meat and vegetable pies in Clark's pie shop, then of the baking of bread in the shop and bakery of Messrs ES Luton and Sons. A final odour to hit the nostrils was that of the manufacture of vinegar at the works of Messrs Plucknett situated in Braunton Road at the Bedminster extremity of North Street. Thus a perambulation along North Street in the 1940s and 50s was indeed an experience to exercise the nasal powers.

During the same period, there were to be heard a number of sounds somewhat unique to North Street. Among these would have been the tramping of feet on the pavements. This sound had two quite distinct sources. First, arising from the hundreds of employees of Messrs WD & HO Wills, walking to and from the Ashton factories each weekday and Saturday mornings. Secondly, on Saturday afternoons during the football season when thousands of supporters made their way on foot to the City Ground (no Ashton Gate Stadium in those days!) to watch their beloved Robins. A somewhat more raucous sound assailed the ears, if passing the Rex Cinema on Saturday evenings. It came from the leather throated commissionaire announcing in a rasping voice that there were two seats available at 'one and nine pence'. Whereupon, there would be a rush forward, from couples who would have been queuing for some time to procure the tickets. Perhaps a more melodious sound would entice the ear later on a Saturday evening coming from the various North Street hostelries, including the Hen and Chicken, the Spotted Cow, the Masonic, the Full Moon and the Star. This arose as patrons rounded off a convivial night's drinking and socialising with spirited renditions of such old favourites as

'Nellie Dean', 'Daisy Daisy' and even 'The Old Rugged Cross'. And many of the local populace made a special perambulation down North Street on Sunday evenings to listen to the band of the Bedminster Corps of The Salvation Army as they marched with flags flying from their open air service in East Street to the Citadel at the end of North Street. But perhaps the most surprising sounds to be heard in North Street in the period in question were the result of the Second World War. First, in the months leading up to the D Day invasion in June 1944, there was to be heard the strange-sounding accents of the many American soldiers – the GIs – from the two Ashton Court encampments, some even billeted in local homes. Then, in the latter stages of the War, the German prisoners of war imprisoned on the same sites, whose native language was indeed a mystery to most locals. In both cases, as first the Americans and then the Germans wandered up and down North Street, their conversations provided the locals with perhaps their first experience of global citizenship.

The third sensory experience to be had in the North Street of the 1940s and 1950s was that of being brought face to face with some unusual sights. At the Ashton end, there was the burnt out shell of the parish church of Saint Francis of Assisi, which had been destroyed in the infamous Good Friday blitz in April 1941. In fact, a regular North Street walker would have seen the present day building arising like a phoenix from the ashes in the years 1951-53. Further along North Street, in the area between Dorset Street and Sion Road, and on the opposite side between Dartmoor Street and Exmoor Street there were large weed-strewn open spaces. These were the sites of houses and premises which, like the church of Saint Francis, had been destroyed during the blitz and commonly referred to as 'bombed sites'. These sites made wonderful play areas for youngsters with little or no regard for modern day concerns with regard to health and safety. A third sight which would have arrested attention, was that of the green number nine double-deck omnibuses, operated by Bristol Tramway and Carriage Company, trundling up and down North Street en route between Ashton and Hanham, with the conductor hanging by one hand on to the open rear platform.

Many of the sensory experiences I have described have long since ceased to be part of the North Street scene. However, the memories they engender are indeed part of those traditions which make North Street a place where members of the local populace can shop, meet, enjoy life together and about which they can reminisce.'

Steve Williamson, whose first train set came from this shop window

## 1950s AND 60s

### SHOPPING WITH MUM – THE TWILIGHT YEARS OF 'THE HOUSEWIFE'
#### BY STEVE WILLIAMSON

 **'Being born in 1950 and an only child, I was not to be left alone when my mother made her three times a week trips to North Street.** Why three times a week? Well like many others we did not own a fridge until the late 50s so food could not be stored as we do today. North Street to me existed from Raleigh Road to Greville Road, unless it was a Friday and we had to pass the Hen and Chicken to access the fresh fish shop which was another 100 yards further on. Although in our household it was not for religious purposes, we always had fish on a Friday.

There must have been times when I could have been left at home. Grandma was there, Dad was on holiday from work, but perhaps it was company for Mum, or exercise for me – whatever, I was always in attendance! Three times a week, as well as of necessity, it was also a social occasion for Mum. Numerous times I was told off for tugging at her hand or shopping basket as she stood and talked or gossiped with those other regular shoppers. The only exception to this was if I was anywhere near Hedley Price (the electrical part of the shop) and could watch the Hornby electric train running around the track in their window. I later became a very proud owner of one of those demonstration models.

Mother was very well known in her regular shops, and there always seemed something for her to chat about. Everybody seemed to know each other; it was a comfortable community, easy going, and free from threat. Shopping in those days was what could be carried by hand, and cars as a means of transport for shopping did not really exist. But, as a teenager, having bought my first 'old banger', when home from college, I would still regularly take Mum to North Street for her shopping. At last it was me in charge and if she spent too much time gossiping, I could beep the horn, still got told off, but to avoid missing a lift home she always came. The spirit and ethos of North Street have never left me. My wife and I are regular shoppers in many of today's shops. Today, I find it is me who meets people to chat or gossip with and often my wife Carol, or Auntie Peg are in the car waiting for me. It has gone full circle and I guess the old habits practised by my mother have never left me. Long may North Street thrive and although there are not the variety of shops that there used to be, the 'social side' of North Street has gone from strength to strength. Long may it continue.'

Pat Hooper at the Southville Deli, once the home of Rite Wools

# 1980s AND 90s

## SHOPPING FOR NECESSITY – AND PLEASURE

### BY PAT HOOPER

 **'It was a different type of shopping in those days.** I didn't do a large weekly shop as there wasn't an Asda or a Sainsburys then, so I tended to buy things as and when I needed them. There was a Fine Fare just past the Hen and Chicken, where the Co-op is now. It was a fairly large store and I did a lot of my main shopping there. I can remember piling all the shopping into the basket under the pushchair to bring it back home.

I also had some shopping delivered by Smith and Hopewell which we always called 'the Cheese Shop'. I would take my list of groceries in to them during the week. This would be delivered on a Friday and I would pay the lady who delivered it. I would also pay weekly into a Christmas club there, so when Christmas arrived I would have a 'free' shop!

My absolute favourite shop was Rite Wools. I think I'm correct in saying that it was where Southville Deli is now. It was a very large shop. The window would have the most wonderful wools and patterns along with garments that had been knitted up. They also sold a small amount of ladies clothing, mostly blouses. The manageress was a very elegant lady with jet black hair and glasses, probably in about her fifties. The knitting patterns would be on a pull-out shelf and you could browse for ages. When I had chosen my pattern, I would spend ages choosing my wool. They would put the wool aside for you for a month so you could go in during the month and just buy a couple of balls of yarn as you needed it. They also sold embroidery threads and almost everything to do with embroidery. I remember I bought my first tapestry kit in there to make up the most wonderful red and black cushion which I still have.

It was a very quiet shopping street then as Wills had closed and there were a lot of charity shops. North Street today is a wonderful vibrant place. It's such a mix of different people and businesses and I like the fact that I can just walk up the road to get a pint of milk, go to the bank, have a meal or go and see a play.'

Anna Bryant outside her children's favourite shop, Paper Village

# EARLY 21ST CENTURY

### LARGE AND SMALL SHOPS – GETTING THE BALANCE RIGHT

BY ANNA BRYANT

 **'I grew up in Bristol and moved to Bedminster in 2004.** At that time I used North Street mostly for its cafés and pubs, with the odd visit to Lion Stores as I was doing up a house. It wasn't until I had my daughter four years ago that I started to discover a whole other daytime life to the street. Before that I could never understand how people could be expected to shop at a butcher's (then Wherlock's) that shut by 2pm on a Saturday. Now I do my best to avoid the crush at Rare Meat and Ashton Fruit Shop on a Saturday by doing my shopping on a week day, although I still get caught out by Wednesday afternoon closing sometimes!

Sometimes I feel like a 1950s housewife when I go out shopping to North Street, visiting the butchers, greengrocers, bakers and other speciality shops. I wouldn't be without the supermarket though for tins, cereals and so on and use both Aldi and Asda. There has been quite a bit of discussion about the threat of supermarkets to North Street's independent shops in the future. From my own experience I think a balance can be achieved. I wouldn't want to give up the quality of local traders' specialities or the convenience of filling the cupboards in one big shop.

I enjoy the sociability of North Street. I always see someone I know when I walk down the street, which enhances my sense of community and belonging. I've felt a part of new businesses that open and have cheered them on, although Mark's Bread has become a bit of a temptation...

I still use the pubs and cafes on North Street, and regularly appreciate having two theatres and a comedy club on the street too. I think we could do with a bigger variety of restaurants though, and then my life will be complete; I need never leave for anything!

My family living in Hotwells can regularly be found over this side of the river using North Street. It makes me feel very lucky to have such a great asset on my doorstep.'

# END NOTE

When we planned this book, our intention was to tell the story of shopping in North Street by exploring the history of its shops. We used a variety of methods, in particular listening to the tales of shop workers and shoppers. Although we were told by numerous people what North Street was like in the days 'when Wills' was still there' and shops were filled to overflowing at lunchtime and after the factory day was done, many of the same people acknowledge that North Street is at last back on its feet again. Furthermore, instead of uncovering stories of rivalry between like-trades, we learned of the interdepency of shopkeepers which continues to this day – of bakers borrowing flour from each other and butchers exchanging sides of bacon – the mutual recognition of the need to survive and prosper.

What does the future hold for North Street? Judging by the comments made by almost all the people interviewed, whether shopkeepers or shoppers, the outlook is good. At the time of writing, empty shops are soon occupied, generally by innovative people determined to bring a new offer to the area, and shops which have opened in the last few years are, in the main, thriving. The threat to North Street from large supermarkets in this part of south Bristol seems to have receded, helped by the intense competion which they are under from the smaller, budget price supermarkets, such as Aldi. There is a growing acceptance by many traders that, rather than posing a threat to independent shops, the several small supermarkets along North Street actually attract customers who may then venture into nearby shops. There is an air of optimism among many of the traders and a growth in confidence of people to use their local shops, demonstrated by the numbers popping in and out of premises all the way along North Street.

Since the start of the twenty first century, this part of south Bristol has become a desirable place to live and the local shops have benefitted as a result. North Street is now very much 'on the map' in Bristol and the wealth of independent shops, as well as other attractions such as 'gastropubs' and the Comedy Box at the Hen and Chicken, as well as the Tobacco Factory, attract people from other parts of the city as well as from further afield. In describing the value that a vibrant shopping street adds to its local community, Paul Wick, manager of the Southville Deli, provides a fitting summary of North Street, Bristol in 2015:

*North Street gives the district a sense of place, a focal point for the community and a reason for people to leave their door and pass their neighbour in the street. They don't have to spend money – just walk around. The place helps keep people in touch. You've only got to listen to chats on the pavement – people bumping into each other, having a conversation and keeping friendships and acquaintances going.*

# GALLERY

The photographs here span over a hundred years. From advertisements to shop interiors, and from shopkeepers to pie-making, they add detail to the stories found elsewhere in this book.

Taken from the corner of Mount Pleasant Terrace, looking along North Street towards Cannon Street. On the left, Willways Dyes (64) later became Brooks cleaners, and is now the Oriental Chef. To the right on the corner with Hebron Road, behind the bread delivery cart, is general dealer Richard Cockram (65, currently the Old Bookshop.) Claude Pullin, grocer, is next door at number 63. On the next corner, with its awning out, is Collard's butchers (57). The Full Moon (currently The Hare) is the three-storey building beyond and then just visible are the gates to the Hebron Burial Ground. The horse and cart are alongside the old cottages that later became Lenthall's, now Carr Power Products (43).

George Hathway in the doorway of his boot shop (208). The Kensitas cigarette poster offers prizes of an 'Austin a day', dating it to c1932. The site is now occupied by a supermarket. Just out of shot to the right is almost certainly the original Georgian Hen and Chicken pub. The dapper man to the left is walking past the off-licence entrance of the rebuilt Edwardian Hen and Chicken.

Mrs Bishop's pre-War music shop at number 74 was taken over as a branch of Duck, Son & Pinker in 1944. The image is from a brochure published in 1948 to celebrate the centenary of the business. However this branch had closed by the mid-1950s, to be replaced by a bakery.

*BEDMINSTER BOYS ACADEMY, near Bristol Conducted by Mr W. Goulstone.*

Bedminster House stood between the current Hebron Road and Melville Terrace. This etching is from the school prospectus issued by William Goulstone, who moved the establishment here in 1829. The prospectus assured parents that there was 'particular regard to the morals and gentlemanly conduct of the Pupils and every effort is made to develop their mental powers & improve their tempers and dispositions.' Goulstone sold Bedminster House in the early 1860s and it was demolished in 1892. The raised pavement ran for a considerable distance along this side of North Street at the time. It has been said that the front doors of numbers 87 and 89, which now have flights of steps, were once level with this terrace.

95

Hassell Robert, 5 Redcliff crescent, New river
Hassell Thomas, Esq. *Mayor*, Mansion house, Queen square, and Bedminster house, North street, Bedminster
Hassell Thomas & Co. *Tanners*, Bedminster
Hassall Thomas, Park villa, near Tyndall's park
Hassall John, 2 Norfolk street

The 1825 Bristol Directory, listing the Mayor's official residence (the Mansion House) and his home in North Street, Bedminster House. Thomas Hassell was thrice sheriff of Bristol and Mayor. Hassell is notorious for attending the first public execution at the New Gaol, that of 18 year-old Thomas Horwood who was hanged in 1821 for throwing a stone at his sweetheart, from the effects of which she died. Hassell had the dead boy's skin tanned and used to bind a book containing the records of the trial.

**149**

William Curtis' painting (c1857) of the rear garden of Dorset House. North Street is on the further side of the building. In the foreground is a young Monkey Puzzle tree, a rarity in Britain at the time, but later to become a very popular Victorian species.

This photo of Haskins' bakery and delivery carts was posed just before the First World War. Ironmongers WJ Owen (117) stood on the corner of North Street and Dorset Street. The row, built around the mid-1880s, was bombed in the Second World War.

Gaywood House block of flats, taken from the junction of Dorset Street and North Street. Constructed by Bristol Corporation in the early 1960s, the flats were built on the bombed land previously occupied by Dorset House and the shops shown on the other page.

When Andrew Nicholls moved here to number 244 with his photographic business Bernard Hunter he found a 'four foot high pile of Dr Hedley Price's medical photographs' along with photographic glass plates of the business's shops. This photograph, printed from one of the glass plates, is undated but was taken before 1920.

The entire window display is devoted to the HP Lung Healer, which 'Touches That Terrible Tickle'. Frank Phillips remembers how 'everyone swore by this cough medicine.'

Note the pole for the tramlines, with the sign 'electric cars stop here if required.' It is not clear if the man is holding back the two children, or making sure they are in the picture.

Scott's Stores (266) after closing time. The photographs is c1920s, not long after the Fry's production line moved from central Bristol to Keynsham. The corner shop is still a general stores (McColl's).

The 1904 building plans for this rank of twenty-six buildings featured just six shops, but by the time of this photograph (c1923-1929) the conversion of number 235 (currently MacDaddy's) from a house to a shop has been completed and next-door is underway. By 2015, only one has remained as a dwelling.

The bombed Hen and Chicken pub seen from Greville Road. A handcart labelled Hen and Chicken Hotel stands in the cobbled yard, and an air-raid shelter sign S points towards North Street.

The Hen and Chicken Hotel, Snack Bar and Restaurant gutted after a bombing raid. The shadow of boot maker George Hathway's demolished shop (208) can be seen beneath the advertisement on the side wall. The Belisha Beacon has lost its globe, but the sign to the swimming baths still clings to the tram pole. The two women wait beneath a sign 'S' for air-raid shelter, whilst a group stand and talk, where behind them the North Street sign has fallen into the rubble. The quality of the glass photographic plate allows us to see that the inscription in the gable names the founder and the then family owner, reading "Jacob Clark 176(?)1 and Martin Clark 1904."

Staff at Hedley Price Photoradio shop (244) c1980. L to R: (front row) Sid Wring, Arthur Curry, Bill King (holding clock), Laurie Phillips; (middle row) Mary Barnes, John Baker, May Nobbs, Margaret Humphries; (back row) Ken Haynes, Vic Lewis, Ernest Dumbleton, Don Loader.

Thomas Lenthall, founder of Lenthalls (37-47). The site is now occupied by Carr Power Products.

John White (right) of The Dinkie (245) discussing cigarette sales with his father, George.

Joan Payne, sporting her brother's cap, in the yard of the family bakers, Pitts (9). Beyond the arch is the junction of North Street and Merrywood Road. The corner shop is number 16, where Joan's friend Aileen Bosley lived. Photograph c1940

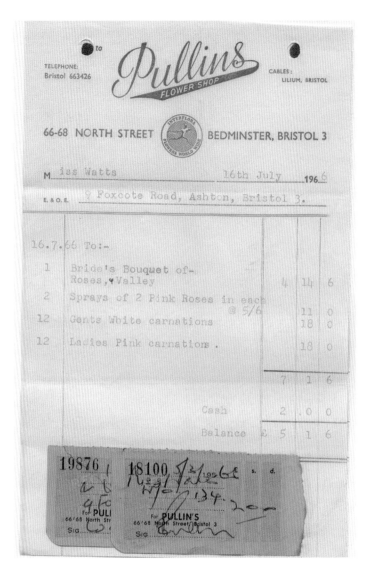

43 & 45, North Street, Bedminster,

BRISTOL, July 8<sup>th</sup> 19**32**

Mr Eley

Cabinét Maker and
Furniture
Dealer

To T. C. DARBY,

Old Furniture
Repaired,
Upholstered and Polished
ANTIQUE FURNITURE NEATLY RESTORED & ALTERED

| Bedroom Suite | 16 | 0 | 0 |
| Bedstead | 3 | 10 | 0 |
| 3 Piece Set. | 7 | 15 | 0 |
| 4 Oak chairs | 4 | 12 | 0 |
| Dining Table. | 2 | 15 | 0 |
| Spring & Wool. | 3 | 15 | 0 |
| | 38 | 7 | 0 |

Paid T C Darby

July 9/1932

With Thanks

With oak dining chairs at around £1, the Eley's fit out their new home in 1932

## Pullins
### FLOWER SHOP

TELEPHONE:
Bristol 663426

CABLES:
LILIUM, BRISTOL

66-68 NORTH STREET — BEDMINSTER, BRISTOL 3

M iss Watts 16th July 196**6**

E. & O. E. 9 Foxcote Road, Ashton, Bristol 3.

16.7.66 To:-

| | | £ | s | d |
| 1 | Bride's Bouquet of Roses, Valley | 4 | 14 | 6 |
| 2 | Sprays of 2 Pink Roses in each @ 5/6 | | 11 | 0 |
| 12 | Gents White carnations | | 18 | 0 |
| 12 | Ladies Pink carnations . | | 18 | 0 |
| | | | 7 | 1 | 6 |
| | Cash | 2 | 0 | 0 |
| | Balance £ | 5 | 1 | 6 |

Invoice from Pullins (66) for June and David Hodge's wedding flowers in the summer of 1966

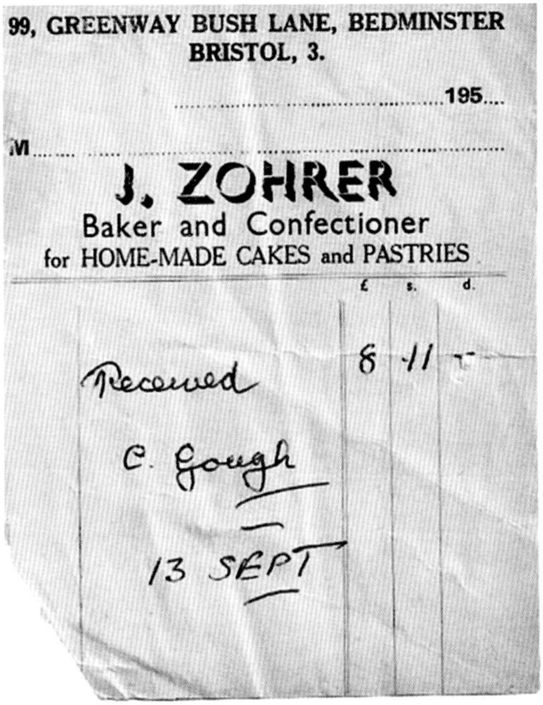

99, GREENWAY BUSH LANE, BEDMINSTER
BRISTOL, 3.

...................................195...

M.........

## J. ZOHRER
### Baker and Confectioner
#### for HOME-MADE CAKES and PASTRIES

| | £ | s. | d. |
|---|---|---|---|

Received          8  11  —

C. Gough

13 SEPT

The receipt for Jill and Trevor Sims' wedding cake, 1968

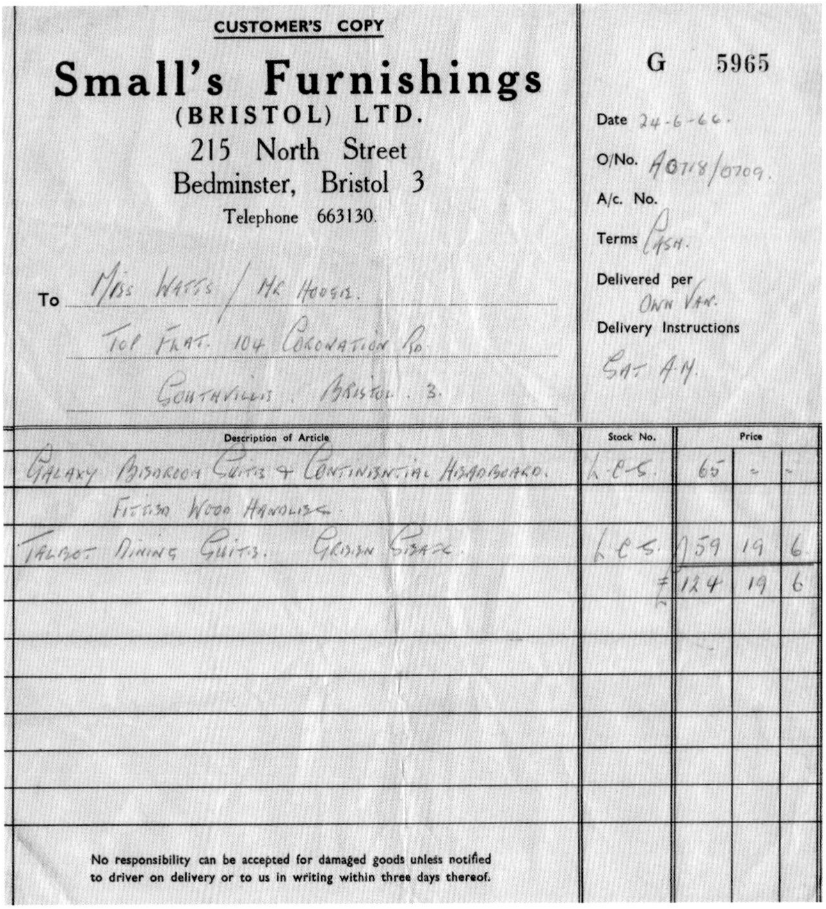

CUSTOMER'S COPY

## Small's Furnishings
### (BRISTOL) LTD.
215 North Street
Bedminster, Bristol 3
Telephone 663130.

G  5965

Date 24-6-66.
O/No. A0718/0709.
A/c. No.
Terms CASH.
Delivered per OWN VAN.
Delivery Instructions
SAT. A.M.

To  Miss Watts / Mr Hodge.
Top Flat. 104 Coronation Rd
Southville  Bristol . 3.

| Description of Article | Stock No. | Price | | |
|---|---|---|---|---|
| Galaxy Bedroom Suite + Continental Headboard. | L.E.S. | 65 | — | — |
| Fitted Wood Handles | | | | |
| Talbot Dining Suite. Grisian Beige. | L.E.S. | 59 | 19 | 6 |
| | £ | 124 | 19 | 6 |

No responsibility can be accepted for damaged goods unless notified to driver on delivery or to us in writing within three days thereof.

David and June (nee Watts) Hodge bought their Talbot dining and Galaxy bedroom suites from Smalls (215) in 1966

# SYLVITA BREAD

Madam,

Do you buy a loaf or do you buy BREAD?

We, as Bakers, can assure you that there is a lot of difference. After supplying the public for more than sixty years with the "staff of life", whether for ordinary consumption in the home, for sandwiches to take to work or for the slice for the hungry child, we have, from the experience of striving for perfection not only attained an exceedingly high quality product, but have been awarded over

### 1,000 CUPS and MEDALS

in open competition throughout the country.

Our interest in the production of this most important food is therefore our foremost concern, and our aim to ensure that the consumer is given complete satisfaction when the call of hunger prevails.

We have now introduced to your area, **SYLVITA BREAD.** Whether you already take our product regularly or not, please let it speak for itself—just try it—for we know that you, as a housewife, are the finest critic we could ever obtain.

Your supplier, in whom we have every confidence, is:—

**E. LUTON & SON LIMITED, BRISTOL, 3**

A new loaf devised by Edward Luton (226) to compete with Mother's Pride and Sunblest. His aim was a bread with 'a silky texture and vitalising.'

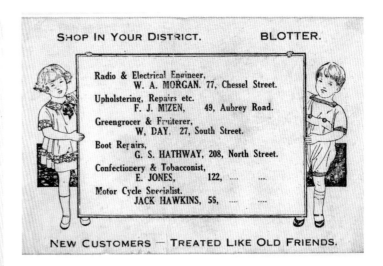

Shopping local, 1930s style. Number 56 was the only one of these three North Street shops to survive wartime bombing.

As well as Meccano, a boy might be bought a Kemex or Electron construction kit from the 1933 Hedley Price catalogue

Hedley Price's photographic shop (246, now Bernard Hunter) hired out cine cameras that were so simple to use that 'success is certain'. The company was well known for the slogans, such as 'Price's Perfect Prints Please', which adorned their shop windows and this 1933 catalogue

Woolly spheres project, Paper Village (200), 2014

Tasty Stop fare (202) in 2013, before closure of the cafe

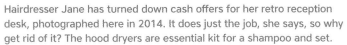

Hairdresser Jane has turned down cash offers for her retro reception desk, photographed here in 2014. It does just the job, she says, so why get rid of it? The hood dryers are essential kit for a shampoo and set.

The start of the production line at Clark's Pies (259); moulds made ready for the pastry case

Filling is added to what will be classic 'Clark's Pies'. The equally popular Clark's pasties are made upstairs.

As the pies come off the line they are sprayed with glaze before being cooked

The pie-team show off the last batch before the regular cleaning of the production line

Conversation being overheard by one of the 'Bedminster Bugs'. Over eighty were painted in 2013 by artists, pupils from local schools and community groups, and mounted on local shops.

Royston Garden News (274) gets a mural during UPFEST 2013. The reference is to Player's Navy Cut cigarettes, and the nautical phrase continues 'and Bristol-fashion.'

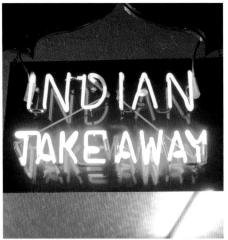

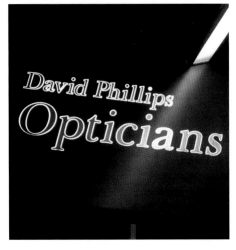

# ACKNOWLEDGEMENTS, SOURCES AND FURTHER READING

**F**irstly, the authors especially wish to thank Chris Bramley and James Dunbar who have been an essential part of the creative team; Chris for his tireless expert advice to help shape our words into a book, and James for his photographer's eye.

Our main sources of information have been the shop-keepers, shop workers and shoppers of North Street. Many were interviewed at length, others contributed in writing and a few have been requoted from other publications. Without them this book would not have been started or completed. We wish to thank the following for their contributions:

Stuart Amesbury, Andy Ball, Ryan Ball, Al Bandali, Barcan Woodward, Solicitors, Mary Barnes, Paul Barnett, Penny Barnett, Simon Bartlett, Edna Beake, Mike Beese, Bob Bennett, Tom Bensted, Kathryn Bewley, Martin Bidder, Brian Billings, Dave Bjelica, Big Issue seller Maria (Bombonica), Peter Brimble, Diana Brown, Anna Bryant, Peter Budd, John Bunt, David Butt, Mary Butt, Cleo Coleas-Canham, Ivan Carter, Linda Carter, Robert Cashman, Alma Chalmers, Bernard Chalmers, Martin Chamberlain, Steve Chivers, Harold Coleman, J (Jeff?) Coleman, Joe Colton, Wendy Colton, Mary Cookson, Jane Cookson, Kevin Cox, Lin Cox, Claire Dadswell, Esme Davidson, Jantzen Derrick, Pat Derrick, Rachel Dowding, Stephen Dowle, June Eley, Ken Eley, Muriel Eley, Phil Eliott, Jim Emsley, Jake Emsley, George Ferguson, Roy Gallop, Anna Gilman, Clive Green, Doreen Hamblin, Andrew Hamer, Dorothy Hamer, Hank Hancock, John Hardingham, Doug Harris, Paul Harris, Vicky Harrison, Carole Hawkes, Alan Hawkins, Jane Hawkins, Steve Hayles, David Hodge, June Hodge, Will Holland, Graham Hopewell, Jack House, Xanthe Ivory, Aileen James, Bruce James, Luke Jarvis, Jeane Johns, Jeff Johnston, Josh and Damon of Garland Zero, Derek Knapman, Nicky Lanfear, John Lenthall, Martyn Lewis, Gordon Luton, Mark Manning, Joan Marsh, Scott Maxwell, John Miles, Sue Mountsevens, Pete Neale, Phyllis Neale, Mark Newman, Jim Nichols, Andrew Nicholls, Joan Nurmeleht, Brian Parsons, Ron Payne, Malcolm Pearce, Valerie Pearce, Lew Pedlar, Frank Phillips, Keith Prested, Roy Pullin, Paul Wick, Ray Bowles, Dean Reed, Gilbert Robbins, Hilary Rogers, Mike Rogers, Mark Rudge, Dave Russell, Aaron Short, Jill Sims, Trevor Sims, Brian Sleeman , Sylvia Sleeman, Mrs E Smith, Mr K L Smith, Mervyn Southway, Gina Stanford, Janet Steele, Margaret Stevenson, Pat Stiles, Kevin Summerill, June (customer in the Tasty Stop), Anne (serving in the Tasty Stop), George Thomas, Barbara Thorn, Peggy Triggle, Mr Tucker, Mr A J (John?)Walker, Barrie Wheeler, Bob Wherlock, John White, Ken Whitehead, Rex Whitlow, Emma Williams, Sheila Williams, Glyn Williams, Steve Williamson, Mary Windell, Vernon Windell, Valerie Wood, Karen Woodley, Pet Wrigglesworth.

In addition to those who opened up their family albums for us, we would like to thank the following individuals and organisations who have loaned images (description or street number in brackets): Memories, Old Photographic Prints, Corn Exchange, Bristol; Malago Society Archives; Bygone Bristol; Bath in Time – Bath Central Library; Weird Old Hattie on flickr.com (North St Snack Bar, Able TV); Fiducia Press (246, Poet's Corner); Tom Osborn (Xanthe); Tom Ford www.whateversleft.co.uk (Paragon Snooker interior); Stephen Dowle (Imperial Carpets); Sally Ilett (Briswool); Rosie Tomlinson (Mike Beese, Mark Rudge, performances in Dinkie, Ashton Fruit Shop and Stafford's Laundrette); Richard Walker (Rex – Adam Faith); Paulbox Photography (UPFEST); Nick Townsend (Tattootime window, Nylon Shop); Myk Garton (North St Green); dusashenka on flickr.com (Rex interior); Dean Marks (Gloucestershire Regiment); Brizzle born and bred on flickr.com (view from Collards, 113-117); Aztec West on flickr.com (Gala Bingo, Collard 2013).

The following are the reference numbers for the images reproduced from the collections of the Bristol Museums, Galleries and Archives, for which many thanks:

Bristol Record Office: all maps, 40221/4, 27545/1-15, 40826-HSG-051, 41242/IM/Ph/4, 9735 and 36203, AC/JS/60a-e, Building Plan 25 folio 77d, Building Plan 43 folio 10d, Building Plan Volume 11102b, Building Plan/Vol 43/34b, Building Plan/Volume 38/76a. Bristol Museums and Art Galleries: K2969/010, M4346, M4353; Hartley Collection 24843, 50, 579, 580, 582.

Many thanks also to Phil Hooper (www.philsballoons.co.uk) for all modern aerial photos; Laura Beaven for her original artwork of shop fronts; and James Dunbar for many of the contemporary images. All other contemporary images, Martin Howard.

We have endeavoured to ensure that the owners of the images used have granted consent for their publication. All reasonable endeavours have been made to ascertain first ownership copyright, but acknowledgment here does not necessarily imply this. The authors have no intention to infringe copyright and will acknowledge copyright holders should they make themselves known to the publisher.

We would also like to thank the following who have gone out of their way to offer support, material, or publicity: Roy Gallop of south Bristol's Fiducia Press; Sheila Hannon from Show of Strength; George Ferguson; Lew Pedlar and Memories of Bedminster; Derek Fisher of Bygone Bristol for his postcard collection; local historian Anton Bantock, with thanks for the loan of a caption; Julia Carver of Bristol Museum and Art Gallery; Peter Insole of Know Your Place; Ben Barker; Ken Fyfe for his very helpful advice following his reading of our draft manuscript; our book designer Joe Burt and publisher Richard Jones of Tangent Press.

Finally, we wish to thank the Better Bedminster Community Chest for their generous publication grant.

Needless to say, all errors are the responsiblity of the authors, who would like to be made aware of corrections and further stories via northstreetshopping@gmail.com

## FURTHER READING AND OTHER SOURCES

Most of the following can be found in the Bristol Central Library collection:
*Remember Bemmy*, journal of the Memories of Bedminster group
Malago Society magazine
Street Directories
Archive copies of the *Bristol Mercury* newspaper
Anton Bantock, *Bedminster* (Tempus Publishing 2004)
David Bolton, *Made in Bristol* (Redcliffe Press 2011)
Bristol and Avon Family History Society Journal 106 (December 2001)
CLASS, *Southville People and Places* (Fiducia Press 2004)
CLASS and Ken Griffiths, *Miners' Memories of the South Bristol Coalfield* (Fiducia Press 2011)
Ronald Cleeve, *My Malago Book* (unpublished, produced for pupils of Parson Street School)
Peter Davey, *Bristol Tramways* (Middleton Press 1995)
B Cottle, *Joseph Cottle and the Romantics* (Redcliffe Press 2008)
B Cottle, *Joseph Cottle of Bristol* (Bristol Branch of the Historical Association 1987)
J Cottle, *Early Recollections*, chiefly relating to the late Samuel Taylor Coleridge (1837)
J Cottle, *Reminiscences of Samuel Taylor Coleridge and Robert Southey* (Houlston & Stoneman 1847)
CE Deming, *Old Inns of Bristol* (Tempus Publishing 2005)
David Eveleigh, *Bristol – The Photographic Collection* (Sutton Publishing 2003)
Caroline Fitton, *Sign Language* (Andre Deutsch 1987)
John Holland, Pat Hooper and Martin Howard, *A Small Corner of Bristol* (Redcliffe Press 2009)
G Lamoine, *Letters from Joseph Cottle to William Wordsworth* 1828 – 1850
John Londei, *Shutting up Shop – The Decline of the Traditional Small Shop* (Dewi Lewis Publishing 2007)
John Lyes, *Bristol's Courts of Law* (Bristol Branch of the Historical Association 2006)
Ross Melnick and Andreas Fuchs, *Dream On: Bristol Writers on Cinema* (New Words 1994)
James and Karia Murray, *Store Front – The Disappearing Face of New York* (Gingko Press 2008)
Will Musgrave, *South Bristol Through Time* (Amberley Publishing 2013)
Alan Powers, *Shop Fronts* (Chatto & Windus 1989)
Helen Reid, *Bristol & Co* (Redcliffe Press 1987)
Mike Taylor and Maggie Shapland, *Bristol's Forgotten Coalfield Bedminster* (South Gloucestershire Mines Research Group 2012)
Leonard Vear, *Bedminster Between the Wars* (Redcliffe Press 1986)
George White, *Tramlines to the Stars* (Redcliffe Press 1995)

Other sources include: online photographic community Flickr; Bristol City Council's Know Your Place website; Google Street View for "then and now" comparisons with the old street views.

# INDEX – SHOPS AND OTHER COMMERCIAL PREMISES

**PLEASE NOTE:** this is not an exhaustive list, but intended to help readers locate the main shops and other premises referred to in the book. Street address number in brackets (**1**) followed by page number/s (*photographs in italics*)

## ANTIQUES AND SECOND-HAND GOODS
Michael's Antiques (**57**) 30, *30*
Rachael's Quality Second-hand Goods (**59**) 30

## BAKERS AND SPECIALIST CONFECTIONERS
Denny's (**226**) 93
Haskins (**115**) *150*
Jordan's (**156**) 108, *108*
Luton and Son (**226**) *49*, 94-5, *160*
Mark's Bread (**291**) 72-73, *73*, 143
Mountstevens (**223**) 56-57, *56*
Occasion Cakes (**281**) 70, *70*
Parsons (**252**) 51, *51*, 83
Peartree Bakery 122
Pitt's (**9**) 22, 24, *24*, 126, *157*
Woofenden's (**268**) 78-9
Zara's Chocolates (**228**) 94
Zohrer's (**292**) 74-5, *75*, *159*

## BANKS
HSBC (**217**) 50
Midland (**217**) 50
NatWest – formerly, National and Provincial (**276**) 77, *79*
Somerset and Wiltshire Trustee Savings Bank 117

## BICYCLE RETAILERS AND REPAIRERS
Garland's Zero G (**11-13**) 25, *25*
Strada (**236**) 86, *86*
Todd's (**68**) 118
Tucker's (**69**) 32
Ware's (**177**) 46

## BUTCHERS
Abraham's (**213**) 50
Bennett's (**253**) 53
Burgess (**238**) 92
DR Butt (**238**) 92
Collard's (**52**) 30-31, *30*, *31*, *147*
Eastman's (**5**) 22
Jenkins (**262**) 84
Lye's (**250**) *51*, *85*, 138
Rare Meat (**250**) 85, 143
Sleeman's (**81, 119**) 40

Tanner's (**213**) 50, 97
Wherlock's (**250**) 87

## CAFÉS/BARS, RESTAURANTS AND OTHER EATERIES
Barry's Café (**257**) 53
Brewery Theatre café/bar (next to **291**) 70
Clarks' Pies (**259**) 63-64, *63*, *64*, 83, *139*, *164*, *165*
Curtis and Bell (**234**) 93
Dimsum (**263**) 53
The Flying Frog (**221**) 50
Four Leaf Clover (**260**) 84
Gino's (**257**) 54, 62
Green Bean Café (**209**) 50
The Lounge (**227-231**) 51-52, *51*, 57
The Old Bookshop (**63-65**) 30, *147*
Madras Express (**223**) 50
Margot May (**36**) 123
Mediterranean (**242**) 91
Oriental Chef (**64**) 118
Pimm's Pizza (**257**) 62
Regency Café (**257**) 53
Reliance Café (**260**) *85*
Savannah (**273**) 54
Souk Kitchen (**277**) 68
Tasty Stop (**202**) 101, *101*, *162*
Teoh's (**280**) 77
Tobacco Factory café/bar (**278**) 9, 17, *68*, 77
Willow Garden (**281**) 70
Zazu's Kitchen (**220**) 97

## CAR AND SCOOTER DEALERS, CAR ACCESSORIES, EXHAUST PIPES, TYRES AND REPAIRS
Anthony's Motors (**100-108**) 112, 113
Bedminster Hand Car Wash and Valet Centre (**2**) 133
Fanatic Scooters (**56-58**) 119
Heathman's (**2**) 133
Motoring Direct (**133-135**) 41, *41*
Regent Tyres (**293**) 70
Sparkes Garage (**100-108**) 113

## CHARITY SHOPS
Barnardo's 104
Cats' Protection League 78
Children's Hospice South West 83
St Peter's 83
Tenovus 83

## CHEMISTS AND HEALTH PRODUCTS
Health Unlimited (**248**) 88, *88*
Hedley Price (**244**) *51*, 89-91, *90*, *91*, 131, *152*, *156*, *161*
Hodder's (**234**) 93-94
Mills and Mills (**263**) 53
Weston's (**234**) 93

## CINEMAS
Ashton Cinema – The Plaza (**275**) 50, 52, 54, 58, 61, 65-67, *66*, 79
The Rex (**19-25**) 22, 25-27, *25*, *26*, *27*, 139
Gala Bingo – see The Rex

## CLOTHING AND SPORTS (INCLUDES OUTFITTERS, HOSIERY AND MILLINERS)
Bandbox (**254**) 113
Bosley's (**22**) 126-127, *126*, *127*
Carlton Perry Gowns (**221**) 50, 55
Clarke's (Cannon Street) 22
Dix (**125**) 42
Dunn's (**127**) *40*
Fisher's (**29**) 27
Keith Pople (**20** and **227-231**) 52, 57-59
Loxton's (**44**) 121
Stuckey's (**36**) *123*
Madame de Ville 117
Rite Wools (**262**) 142
Edgar Williams (**40**) 121
Joshua Williams (**237**) *60*

## DRAPERS, WOOLS, CRAFT SUPPLIES
Batten's (**247**) 53
Miles (Cannon Street) 130
Nylon Shop (**8**) 132, *132*
Paper Village (**200**) 102-103, *102*, *103*, *162*

Rite Wools (**262**) 142
Stringer's (**272**) 78

## ELECTRICAL GOODS
Eddy's Domestic Appliances (**279**) 68, 69, *69*

## ESTATE AGENTS
Allen and Harris (**261**) 53
Andrews (**215**) 50
Connell's (**243**) 53
CJ Hole (**268**) 79
Northwood (**271**) 54
Ocean (**275**) 54, 65, 67

## FRIED FISH SELLERS AND FISHMONGERS
Dollery's (**267**) 54
Eli Bence (**223**) 50
Enid's (**181**) 46, *47*
Fishminster (**267**) 54
Iles (**181**) 70
Kwan's (**34**) 123, *129*
Mak's (**34**) 123
Thompson's (**181**) 46-47
Tuck's (**60**) 118
Tucker's (**283**) 62, 70
Webber's (**262**) 54
Wilmott's (**60**) 118, 125
Worgan's (**159**) 43-44

## FURNITURE MANUFACTURERS AND RETAILERS, UPHOLSTERERS AND CARPET RETAILERS
Bobby Burns (**196**) 105-106, *105*, *106*
Darby's (**43-45**) 23
Fryer's (**77**) 34
Helibeds (**206**) 100
Imperial Carpets and Beds (**275**) 67, *67*
In Recovery (**56-58**) 118
Lenthall's (**37-47**) 23, *28*, *29*, 156
David Levy and Sons (**215**) 50
McDavid's (**11**) 27
Second-Address (**56-58**) 118
Small's Furnishings (**215**) 50, *159*
South West Upholstery (**196**) 105,

# INDEX – PEOPLE, PLACES AND EVENTS